HIT REVERSE

BY JASH DHOLANI
(@OLDBOOKSGUY)

Published by Aristo Books

ISBN: 9798302922861

For information regarding special discounts for bulk purchases, please contact Aristo Books at jashdholani.z@gmail.com

Cover Design by Nishi Agarwal (@medleybynishi)

TABLE OF CONTENTS

PART TWO: B FOR BALLS

PART THREE: C FOR CIVILIZATION

INTRODUCTION

Ideas are weapons. An idea can pierce foes like an arrow pierces predators. An idea can catch attention like a fishnet catches dinner. An idea can cut through confusion like an axe cuts through trees. A big idea can convincingly end a debate the way a big bomb can convincingly end a war. Ideas are weapons. Perhaps the reason you cannot pierce, cut, and blow through your problems is that you're short on weaponry.

But worry not. You're now holding an arsenal shaped like a book.

Inside this book are ideas that will burn off your confusion, shield you from propaganda, blow through your mental blocks, guide you through mazes, and give you the firepower you need to face down the modern world and its tests, tricks, and treachery.

I focus on old books because you already know what the new books say. Even if you haven't read all of them, you've breathed in their ideas through the air, through conversation, through music, through films. It is in old books where forgotten but effective weapons lie. It is in old books where we find ideas that time could not eliminate. It is in old books where we find writers unconcerned with the risk of cancellation. And so it is to old books we turn.

HIT REVERSE has 5 thematic clusters, divided into 5 parts:

- A for ART
- B for BALLS
- C for CIVILIZATION
- D for DEBATABLE
- E for EUREKA!

The headings are the way they are because I wanted a structure that was fresh and fun, while also being self-explanatory. Further, this structure gives me scope for future expansion. F for...G for...

So, my dear friend. Get ready to think. Get ready to reflect. Get ready to Hit Reverse.

Veer Bhogya Vasundhara
(The brave shall inherit the Earth)

PART ONE

A FOR ART

1

THE ROMAN WAY TO BUILD

De Architectura, 30 B.C.

Julius Caesar employed him. Augustus Caesar patronized him. Da Vinci copied his designs. His name was Vitruvius, and he wrote a text that is now history's oldest surviving architecture book:

De Architectura (30 B.C.)

The Parthenon. The Acropolis. The Colosseum. Each year, millions of visitors flock to these ancient sites. Why does classical Greek and Roman architecture still inspire—and mystify? Vitruvius, a man who lived in Ancient Rome and idolized Ancient Greece, had a front-row seat to that age and the structures they built.

What did he see?

What lessons did he set down for posterity?

Let's find out...

Lesson 1: An architect should be a polymath.

Vitruvius writes:

"He should have a literary education, be skilful in drawing, knowledgeable about geometry and familiar with a great number of historical works, and should have followed lectures in philosophy attentively; he should have a knowledge of music, should not be ignorant of medicine, should know the judgements of jurists and have a command of astronomy and of the celestial system."

Architecture is a specialist domain today—like most other domains. But Vitruvius argues that an architect should be a generalist. He should have a sweeping command of disciplines from law to astronomy to music. Here's why: an architect has to solve an exceedingly broad set of problems. He must structure human life without restricting it. He must provide for present use cases while ensuring the building can be adapted for new uses in the future. He must know biology because he must understand which buildings keep its inhabitants healthy and which ones make them sick. He must know music because it will teach him harmony and flow. He must know astronomy so his buildings are compatible with seasonal shifts in light, temperature, and humidity. And that's why an architect must be a generalist.

Lesson 2: Before constructing a new city, conduct the "Animal Sacrifice Test."

Animal sacrifice is often used as an example of the barbarity of past civilizations. In *De Architectura,* Vitruvius makes a compelling case for why animal sacrifice *must* be carried out on prospective sites for new cities:

"We must resort to the ancient method more and more; for our ancestors sacrificed animals grazing on the sites where they wanted to build towns, and examined their livers; if, according to the first test, the livers were bluish and damaged, they sacrificed other animals because they were not certain whether the livers had been damaged by some disease or by bad alimentation. After they had made a number of tests and demonstrated that the consistency and solidity of the livers resulted from the local water and pasturage, they set up their fortifications on that spot; if, however, they kept on finding that the livers were infected, they would deduce that the supply of water and food occurring naturally in these areas would be just as damaging to human beings, and so they moved on and changed to another area in search of conditions which were healthy in every respect."

Vitruvius suggests that some areas might look healthy to the naked eye, and yet have toxins seeped in the very ground. Now you can replace the animal sacrifice test with other proxy tests, but ultimately *we* are animals, made of blood and bone and skin, and the best predictor for how the land will affect us is to study how it affects *other* animals...

Lesson 3: Learn from the human body.

Consider the insane versatility of the human body. It can run, walk backward, throw, kick, climb, sculpt, punch, swing, carve, jump, and swim. Imagine how precise the measurements and proportions of our body have to be for us to produce such a stunning range of movements. And yet we don't appreciate the geometric beauty of the human body. Vitruvius did. He wrote: "No temple can be designed rationally...unless its elements have precisely calculated relationships like those of a well-proportioned man."

Vitruvius explains how the Greeks used the proportions of the male body to invent the Doric style in temple architecture:

"When they wanted to set up the columns in the temple, they had no proportional system appropriate to them, and so, trying to find out what procedures could be adopted to ensure that the columns would be capable of bearing the loads and that the beauty of their appearance would be assured, they measured the sole of a man's foot and applied it to his height. When they discovered that a man's foot is a sixth of his height, they applied that unit to the column and allocated six times the diameter they had established for the bottom of the shaft to its height, including the capital: that is why the Doric column began to exhibit the proportions, strength and grace of the male body in buildings."

And then the ancient Greeks used the proportions of the *female* body to invent the Ionic style of temple architecture:

"Some time later they built a Temple of Diana; searching for a look for the new order, they used the same plans, adapting them to feminine gracefulness...On the capital they placed volutes at right and left like graceful curls hanging down from the hair; they decorated the fronts with convex mouldings and runs of fruit arranged like hair, and sent flutes down the whole trunk like the folds in the robes traditionally worn by married women. And that is how they developed two different types of columns: one which looked naked, undecorated and virile, the other characterized by feminine delicacy, decoration and modularity. In fact, later builders, becoming more sophisticated with regard to elegance and subtlety of judgment and, delighting in more graceful modules, established seven diameters as the height for the Doric column and nine for the Ionic: the latter, which the Ionians built first, is therefore called the Ionic."

The mirror can do more than help you take selfies. It can teach you proportion, angles, and the mathematical underpinnings of beauty...

Lesson 4: Learn from nature.

Many old buildings become narrower as they rise up. Vitruvius notes that the Ancient Greeks learnt to build like this by observing trees. Pines, Firs, and Cypresses become narrower as they rise because that's how you get optimal weight distribution. For the observant, nature is a prolific teacher.

The Ancient Romans didn't stop at trees. They perfected the sound engineering of their public theaters by noticing pond ripples. Vitruvius explains how:

"The voice is like a flowing breath of air...It moves in infinite concentric circles, just as when a stone is dropped in standing water, innumerable expanding circles of ripples develop and spread out from the centre as widely as they can, unless interrupted by the narrowness of the pond or some other obstacle. And so when they are interrupted by obstacles, the first ripples turn back and disturb the pattern of those that follow them...

"In the same way the voice diffuses itself in concentric circles, but while the circles in water move horizontally on a flat surface, the voice not only expands outwards horizontally but also rises in regular stages. Therefore, as with the pattern of ripples in water, so too with the voice: when no obstruction blocks the first wave, it does not interfere with the second nor with those following, but they all reach the ears of the spectators in the lowest and highest seats without rebounding...

"Therefore the ancient architects, taking their lead from nature, designed the tiers of seats in theaters on the basis of their investigations into the rising of the voice, and tried, with the help of mathematicians' principles and musical theory, to devise ways in which any voice uttered onstage would arrive more clearly and pleasantly at the ears of the spectators."

Lesson 5: We need an Olympics Of The Mind...

Vitruvius had a complaint against his beloved Greeks: they didn't celebrate authors as much as athletes. Ancient Greece valued feats of physical excellence so much that they organized annual games, including but not limited to The Olympics, to celebrate them. Alexander The Great's father was a celebrated Olympic horse-rider. Vitruvius wrote that feats of intellectual excellence deserve just as much focus, if not more. After all, athletes "merely make their bodies stronger by training," but great authors strengthen their entire civilization by saving important ideas for posterity.

2

ARISTOTLE'S CRASH COURSE ON
CREATIVITY

The Art of Rhetoric, 4th century B.C. // Poetics, 335 B.C.

Aristotle was born in the classical age of Greece, studied under Plato, and became a private tutor to Alexander The Great. Aristotle is among history's greatest polymaths—66% of his work is lost but go through what remains and you get splendid treatises on language, biology, economics, and a dozen other subjects. There are hundreds of entry points into Aristotle...in this chapter we'll look into his lessons, both profound and practical, for artists of today:

Aristotle was dissing modern art 2550 years ago: "If an artist were to cover a surface with the finest and most beautiful colors at random, it would provide the viewer with less pleasure than a simple outline of an object." Today you see artworks that are a mishmash of different materials, styles, and ideas. Think of Jackson Pollock's drip paintings: *no* coherence, *some* exuberance, *all* noise. Aristotle says the "most beautiful colors at random" will always be less beautiful than a simple little sketch. The visual arts—from painting to sculpture—are in the business of representing the geometry (and spirit) of life. Life exhibits patterns, beauty, and propulsive movement towards goals. Art must capture this, instead of elevating Randomness to the stature of a God.

Aristotle on why proportions REALLY matter: "**Beauty must have size as well as order**. Because of this no animal can be beautiful if it is too small, since we would pass over it quickly, unable to observe it, or enormously large—say a thousand miles long—since we would not be able to observe and take in the whole thing all at once. Just as physical objects and living organisms should possess an appropriate size and be able to be comprehended in a coherent way, so too with plots." Art—words, symbols, and everything in between—is fundamentally for, by, and of humans. Skewed sizes, from too little to too large, are *inhuman.*

Aristotle on why writers should aim for *maximum manageable complexity*: "What should matter to the writer is...the principle that a longer plot is usually better and more beautiful, provided that it can still be held in the memory all at once."

Here's Aristotle bemoaning how special effects were spoiling ancient Greek drama. The more things change, the more they remain the same: "To create pity and fear with spectacle and special effects has little to do with the art of writing and more with how much money the producer spends on stagecraft. Those performances that use mere spectacle to evoke amazement and not fear have nothing to do with tragedy."

Movies would vastly improve if the scriptwriters were made to read Aristotle first. Here's an Aristotle on how male and female courage cannot look the same: "A character can be courageous, for example, but it would be inappropriate for a female character to be courageous or clever in the same way as a man." Contemporary dogma says that all differences between males and females are social constructs except for some trifling genital distinctions. This dogma flies in the face of every single human interaction you'll ever have but it still has serious currency in the modern world. Aristotle disagrees, and he's right. To equate male courage with female courage is to eviscerate the value and *uniqueness* of both.

Aristotle on the most important thing in storytelling: "The most important thing in storytelling is to be clear, but not too ordinary." Be maximally interesting without flying off the guardrails of clarity.

Borrow phrases from other languages but do it sparingly. Aristotle: "Language is impressive and distinguished if you use words that are uncommon—by which I mean foreign words, metaphors, lengthened forms, and all other more elevated usage. But if your whole story is written like this it's going to be nothing but riddles or gibberish..."

Aristotle talks about the "mixture of the special and the ordinary" all writers should aim for: "What a writer should aim for in language is a mixture of the special and the ordinary. Elevated words—like foreign terms, metaphors, ornamental words—make your language stand out and give it a certain dignity. Everyday language, on the other hand, will give your writing clarity."

Aristotle writes that imitation is the foundation of art: "Writers are imitators, just like painters or other kinds of visual artists. Logically therefore writers must imitate things either as they are (or were), as people say and think they are, or as they ought to be." Today artists carry in their heart an unconscious bias against imitation. In this postmodern climate, the value of an artwork comes down to how novel it is. Therefore you get buildings bent out of shape, stream-of-consciousness books with no narrative coherence, and paintings that are vivid, wild, and without vision.

Run away from all imitation and you end up in a creepy place that's uncanny, unstitched, unhinged. A graveyard of meaning. C.S. Lewis, writing thousands of years later, added to Aristotle's argument: "In literature and art, no man who bothers about originality will ever be original: whereas if you simply try to tell the truth (without caring twopence how often is has been told before) you will, nine times out of ten, become original without ever having noticed it."

3

DOES BEAUTY MATTER WHEN THE BOMBS START FALLING?

Learning In Wartime, 1939

C.S. Lewis, the creator of *Narnia*, addressed a crowd of Oxford students in 1939. The world was on the cusp of the second world war. An ominous chill hung in the air. The students of philosophy, history, and the arts felt like their pursuits were senseless in the coming world of trench warfare, fighter planes, and political chaos. C.S. Lewis spoke directly to this anxiety. He showed them how beauty and truth always matter—even when the bombs start falling. Let's dig in.

To be concerned with truth, beauty, and culture as one's nation fights a war—is this equivalent to "fiddling while Rome burns?" Lewis' reply: "The war creates no absolutely new situation; it simply aggravates the permanent human situation." The *permanent* human situation is endless strife, chaos and pain. C.S. Lewis: "Human life has always been lived on the edge of a precipice. Human culture has always had to exist under the shadow of something infinitely more important than itself." *Yet* culture breaks out.

If we waited for peace to create art the first cave painting would still not be made. There's always some "imminent danger" looking more important than culture. Lewis: "If men had postponed the search for knowledge and beauty until they were secure, the search would never have begun."

C.S. Lewis considers the difference between insect life and human Life: "The insects have chosen a different line: they have sought first the material welfare and security of the hive, and presumably they have their reward. Men are different." We demand not just mere continuity but variety, growth, and adventure. C.S. Lewis on why humans are a truly unique species: "Men propound mathematical theorems in beleaguered cities, conduct metaphysical arguments in condemned cells, make jokes on scaffolds, and comb their hair at Thermopylae. This is not panache; it is our nature."

C.S. Lewis fought in WW-I. He saw that right on the "front line," soldiers didn't talk of the "allied cause" or "progress of the campaign." They were instead concerned with stories, myths, and fateful open-ended questions. They desired "aesthetic satisfactions." If they couldn't "read good books," they read "bad ones."

CS Lewis on why ideas matter: "Good philosophy must exist, if for no other reason, because bad philosophy needs to be answered. The cool intellect must work not only against cool intellect on the other side, but against the muddy heathen mysticisms which deny intellect altogether." By "muddy heathen mysticisms," I think he means postmodernism. Even though the word hadn't been coined yet, C.S. Lewis must have felt the chilly winds of relativism blowing in his direction in 1939. He could see the future: an age where men believed nothing, held no standards, and had minds weak as twigs lost in a storm. Trying to live like a relativist is like trying to walk without gravity. Coherent acts are only possible in the polarity of good and bad. We can argue about the position of the poles, but if we *erase* the poles, then we'll be lost in a maddening universe with no up or down.

Lewis says that the soul feeds on truth and beauty like the body feeds on food: "God makes no appetite in vain. We can therefore pursue knowledge and beauty in the sure confidence that by so doing we are either advancing to the vision of God ourselves or indirectly helping others to do so."

Lewis on why we must study the past: "Not that the past has any magic about it, but because we cannot study the future, and yet need something to set against the present, to remind us that the basic assumptions have been quite different in different periods." The past saves you from the myopia of the present.

The past also provides immunity from new-age B.S. Lewis: "A man who has lived in many places is not likely to be deceived by the local errors of his village; the scholar has lived in many times and is therefore...immune from the great cataract of nonsense that pours from the press of his own age."

Bottomline: Don't wait for spare time to know what you want to know and to chase what you want to chase. C.S. Lewis: "The only people who achieve much are those who want knowledge so badly that they seek it while the conditions are still unfavorable. Favorable conditions never come."

4

HOW TO BE A GENIUS

Genius: The Natural History of Creativity, 1995

At his time of death, Hans Eysenck was the most cited man in psychology. He became a posthumous target for cancellation due to his research on racial differences in IQ. For a mainstream researcher, he wrote on surprisingly esoteric subjects (*"Astrology — Science or Superstition?"*) He published a book on genius in 1995, 2 years before his death. It's a great book about the psychological cocktail that leads to brilliant ideas. Dig in.

Geniuses need a big ego. *Genius* has the same root word as *genie*. But if a genius is to perform magic like a genie, then he cannot operate by the same laws of reality as everyone else. He must risk, tinker, and experiment. But what about all the social blowback? That's where the big ego buffers him. Eysenck: "Your typical genius is a fighter." To drill down, a genius's big ego manifests as arrogance, ambition, and persistence.

Arrogance. Catherine Cox studied the childhood of 300 famous geniuses of history and noted that they widely shared an "innate assurance of superior ability." Life outcomes are sometimes self-fulfilling prophecies. Both negative and positive priming works. **Lesson**: Prime yourself carefully. Better an inner voice too arrogant than too self-effacing.

Ambition. Arrogance is not enough. Intelligence is not enough. You also need an overpowering "desire to excel." W. J. Sidis was reading Homer in original Greek at 3. Hawksworth tested 170 on an IQ test at 11. Jocelyn Lavin was a Classical Music prodigy at 9. They all failed to achieve anything spectacular in life. They had all the intelligence in the world, and perhaps a healthy amount of self-esteem, but lacked what Eysenck calls "significant aims." They lacked ambition. **Lesson**: You need to cultivate a *hunger* for triumphs.

Persistence. To the degree that the genius is acting on uncommon insights, his "battle against orthodoxy" will be endless. The group-thinking NPCs will screech, scream, and pelt stones. You need a thick skin. Eysenck labels it "ego strength." It's all important to have the "inner strength" to resist "popular pressure." Nietzsche had to self-publish his books as they barely sold any copies. He persisted and arguably became history's most influential thinker. Catherine Cox wrote that persistence might even be more important than intelligence: "High but not the highest intelligence, combined with the greatest degree of persistence, will achieve greater eminence than the highest degree of intelligence with somewhat less persistence."

A genius' arrogance, ambition, and persistence give him psychological ammunition to push through difficulties. But how exactly does he get path-breaking ideas? Well, Eysenck argues, the geniuses are low-key schizophrenic.

You are sane because you have "latent inhibition." That's a term for your brain's tendency to ignore *most* sensory input and pay attention to *some* things *only*. Well, check this out: both schizophrenics and creatives *lack* latent inhibition. Neurochemically, their brains have high dopamine and low serotonin secretions. Simply put: their brain takes in more data. Thus they have vastly more dots to connect. Their neurochemistry helps them not only collect more dots, but also connect them in less obvious ways. Eysenck writes that they *see* "unusual associations" between "ideas, memories and images."

Aristotle had access to no neurochemistry laboratories, but his exposure to the high society of Ancient Greece (he was Plato's student and Alexander the Great's tutor) led him to a remarkably similar conclusion thousands of years ago: "No great genius has ever been without some madness."

The same neural pathways that led John Nash to write a Nobel Prize winning paper at 23 also condemned him to 30 years of schizophrenia. He says: "I wouldn't have had good scientific ideas if I had thought more normally." Sometimes, you pay a heavy price for your gift. **Takeaway**: Expose yourself to more disciplines, more worldviews, and more data. Carry concepts and metaphors from one domain to another. See what happens. Don't go mad.

Geniuses are also particularly skilled at marshaling their unconscious resources. The conscious brain is great for survival. It uses linear logic to drill through problems. But it's useless for creative breakthroughs. For that, you need non-linear leaps of the unconscious. Throughout history, great geniuses have used their unconscious to catapult themselves to stunning eureka moments. How?

Ironically, consciously working very hard on a problem is the first step to unlocking your unconscious. Emotional investment is key. Poincaré, a French polymath, was nicknamed "The Last Universalist" due to the *sheer range* of his interests. His papers set up the foundations for modern chaos theory, quantum mechanics, and special relativity. Here's how he worked. He'd launch a "systematic attack" on his mathematical problems with great intensity and then he would take a break. He'd go on "geological excursions" or move to a villa by the sea. While he consciously lounged around, rested, and did nothing, his unconscious was hard at work. When he finally returned to work, solutions appeared out of nowhere. Here's how he put it: "All of a sudden the decisive idea presents itself to the mind. It might be said that the conscious work has been more fruitful because it has been interrupted and the rest has given back to the mind its force and freshness."

Another way to tap into your unconscious: trusting your intuition. Your intuition is the sneak appearance of your unconscious in waking life. Newton and Kepler infamously "fudged" their data to hide discrepancies and back their pet theories. Their intuition told them their theory was correct no matter what the data said. Eysenck writes: "Usually the genius is right, of course, and we may in retrospect excuse his childish games."

Bonus: Geniuses also select the right problem. Eysenck: "Often the most creative act is the selection of the problem!" A genius intellect can be wasted on the wrong problem. A problem may be too little for a genius—or unsolvable. A genius must pick an extremely hard problem that's nevertheless "soluble at the present time." Aim high but don't invade Russia in winter.

5

RAGE, RAGE AGAINST MODERN ARCHITECTURE

The Architecture of Servitude and Boredom, 1981

Something is off about modern architecture. But what, exactly? And what to do about it? Russell Kirk took on these questions in a brilliant essay, and offered some great answers:

Kirk's central insight: Certain states of mind will create certain forms of architecture. The converse is true too—architecture creates certain states of mind. Contemporary architecture bores us and promotes servility.

When Kirk sees modern architecture, he sees a "ghastly monotony." An egalitarian and international style flattens all local variety.

Kirk argues modern architecture promotes servility because it *imposes* a style on us that we hate. People overwhelmingly prefer classical architecture, and yet soulless and bland buildings keep going up. A 2009 YouGov survey found 3 out of 4 people prefer traditional buildings over the glassy contemporary eyesores, but have you noticed any change around you? Like slaves, we apparently have no say in the matter.

How to build, instead? Kirk gives 4 broad principles.

Principle One: Build to the humane scale. What is the point of housing people "efficiently" if they hate the walk back home from the bus? A building's height, a block's density, and everything else must serve human interests first.

Principle Two: Nurture roots, don't hack them. Architecture should make people "feel at home." People feel at home in surroundings where there's continuity and slow change, and not daily upheavals.

Principle Three: Put the common good over profit. People prefer it when old neighborhoods and landmarks are repaired and maintained. But there's much more profit in bulldozing it all and building new—and often worse—buildings from scratch.

Principle Four: Don't force abstractions on people. Procrustes, a figure from Greek myth, made his guests sleep in an iron bed. If longer than the bed, he would hack off their legs until they fit. If shorter, he would cruelly stretch them. This is what modern architecture does.

For contemporary architecture, the starting point is not humans but some abstraction. That is, a metaphorical iron bed. Architecture should serve people's "long-established" customs and preferences. People aren't meant to serve architecture's alien customs and fads.

Architects must stop putting abstractions, commercial interests, and the cult of the new ahead of the people who use their buildings. Our built environments are where we live, do our work, build our families, and chase our dreams—and we deserve better.

6

THE MYSTERY OF HUMOR

The Mating Mind, 2000

Geoffrey Miller's explanation for why humans evolved the ability to crack jokes will blow your mind.

Let's first consider randomness in the animal kingdom. In *The Mating Mind* (2000), Geoffrey Miller writes that when scientists "jangle their keys," lab rats go into random and unusual "convulsions." When moths are chased by bats, they produce an "extraordinarily unpredictable range of evasive movements, including tumbling, looping, and power dives." When escaping a fox, a rabbit doesn't take the "shortest escape route." Instead, it tends to "zigzag erratically."

What are the rats, moths, and rabbits doing? They're using randomness as a shield against being hunted by predators. Creative, *random* movement makes their escape more *likely*.

Engineers program fighter planes to move slightly randomly when evading a guided missile. Tennis players are told to "mix it up when they serve and return shots."

Olympic athletes are tested randomly to ensure they can't dope.

Time for a quick detour through an ancient myth. When his enemies tried to capture him, Proteus, a Greek God, escaped "by continually, unpredictably changing from one form into another— animal to plant to cloud to tree." He survived by becoming *random.*

This "protean behaviour" occurs everywhere in nature. When children *play* or kittens *wrestle*, they're honing their *protean* skills. They're *practicing* unpredictability.

Humans spend more than a $100 billion each year funding, playing, and watching sports. What are sports but a battle of protean skills? You have to predict the opponent's next move but keep your own next move unpredictable.

Miller argues that human creativity—manifesting via songs, books, and *humor*—is nothing but advanced protean behavior. Creativity depends on a "rapid, unpredictable generation of highly variable alternatives." Music, narrative, and art that is totally predictable is not *considered* creative—we demand creativity be protean.

Humor is impossible without a sprinkle of protean unpredictability. Humor shows your thoughts and stories are "fascinatingly unpredictable." Being unpredictable to your predators, enemies, and competitors is a big advantage. Hence, humor is *attractive.*

Human art forms like humor, music, and literature may look unique, but they're outgrowths of protean talents we *share* with other animals. Randomness—and its benefits—explain why we value apparently "useless" pursuits like sports, creative works, and a sense of humor.

7

WHY WRITERS MUST STUDY EVIL

The Problem of Evil in Fiction, 1980

Orson Scott Card remains the only man to win the Nebula and Hugo awards back to back in *consecutive* years. You may know him by his novel *Ender's Game*. He was a deeply religious man who nevertheless couldn't deny that there was something sexy about evil. How should a storyteller affirm the moral imperative to do good while taking into account the appeal of evil? Here's how Orson Card dealt with, and resolved, this tension in a timeless lecture:

Orson Scott Card was a "radically orthodox" Mormon. This limited what he could do as a fiction writer. He couldn't write salacious stories or celebrate debased characters. And yet he knew that the presence of evil makes a story "intrinsically more interesting." This made Orson a "two-headed animal." Yes, it was his duty to oppose evil. But to write great stories, he also had to *understand* evil, *depict* evil, and to even give it a *fair* hearing.

People *treat* stories as a necessity, not a luxury. The soviet authorities maintained an iron grip on what people read. To be caught with the wrong book was to risk prison, decades of slave labor, torture, and death. Yet people devised the "samizdat system." They would copy, by hand, dissident books and pass them around at grave risk. Orson: "Even in the darkest times, there were those who would risk their lives in order to read good fiction and pass it on." Real people risked real lives to...read about the made-up lives of made-up people? Why?

Because the best of fiction is literally false but symbolically true. It uses made-up people and non-existent events to explore and understand eternal questions that haunt the hearts of men. Great fiction uses lies to get to the truth, and it's this truth that people are after.

Orson Scott Card: "Evil is more entertaining than unrelenting goodness because any depiction of life without evil is a lie. Now, fiction is made up, but it is not all lies. Or rather, out of the sum of his lies the author's view of truth inevitably emerges, and if the writer has wrought skillfully, some portion of his view of the world will remain with the reader, changing and shaping him."

Evil turns stories into useful warnings: "It is not because the characters do evil that we find them interesting. We identify with them because we recognize both their good and evil desires in ourselves, and through their acts we learn the consequences of our own as yet unmade decisions." Better see through, and live through, the fallout of a terrible act in fiction than in real life.

As Alfred North Whitehead said: "The purpose of thinking is to let our thoughts die instead of us." The purpose of fiction is to let our favorite characters get hurt so we can learn the lesson and avoid the pain ourselves.

Fiction has limits in space and time; it has borders that life lacks. Therefore, Orson Scott Card said, it's "easier to learn from fiction than from life." Easier to extract lessons from contained stories than from the maddening sprawl of life.

Finally, Orson Scott Card lays out the duties for the writer, censor, and reader.

The writer's duty: to be a "lover of goodness and a student of evil." The censor's duty: to remember that "showing evil is not necessarily advocating it." The reader's duty: to take responsibility for a "well-balanced intellectual and emotional and aesthetic diet."

8

10 THOUGHTS ON BEAUTY FROM JORDAN PETERSON

The Maps Of Meaning, 1999

12 Rules For Life, 2018

Jordan Peterson says you should make one thing in your life as beautiful as you can. This will be a direct "invitation to the divine."

Beauty is absolutely terrifying to people because it highlights the ugly.

Modern architecture saves costs but destroys the soul: "Hell is a place of drop ceilings, rusted ventilation grates, and fluorescent lights; the dismal ugliness and dreariness and general depression of spirit that results from these cost-saving features no doubt suppresses productivity far more than the cheapest of architectural tricks and the most deadening of lights saves money. Everyone looks like a corpse under fluorescents."

Great art will "invade your life and change it." You should let this happen. JP: "Buy a piece of art. Find one that speaks to you and make the purchase."

Think of art as a "window into the transcendent." Art lets the light in.

Art is not a luxury but a core need. We use art to "unite ourselves psychologically" and establish "productive peace" with others.

Jordan Peterson on how we live by beauty: "We live by beauty. We live by literature. We live by art. We cannot live without some connection to the divine—and beauty is divine—because in its absence life is too short, too dismal, and too tragic."

Beautiful ideas are tools: "A good theory lets you use things—things that once appeared useless—for desirable ends. In consequence, such a theory has a general sense of excitement and hope about it."

Why religious buildings are beautiful: "If you're going to house the ultimate ideal, you build something beautiful to represent its dwelling place."

Art is not decoration. It's exploration. It is wrong to think that art should be "pretty and easily appreciated." Great art is always a noble "challenge" because it actually retools our perception. Great artists "train people to see."

9

FROM EARTH-CULTS TO
SKY-CULTS

Sexual Personae, 1991

Dostoevsky wrote in a private letter that art is always faithful to the reality of its time. A work of art cannot help but reflect the values of its era. In *Sexual Personae*, Camille Paglia uses two ancient works of art to talk about the trajectory of human civilization.

Venus of Willendorf	Nefertiti
(25,000 years old)	(4,000 years old)

Here's the analysis:

The Venus of Willendorf shows an overweight and amorphous female figure. She's a fertility Goddess. Nefertiti shows a sharp, painfully austere female face with a disproportionately big head. Paglia: "The head is swollen to the point of deformity."

Paglia believes that human societies were initially "Earth-cults" and later became "Sky-cults." Earth-cults are dependent on mother nature and hence worship her. They benefit from her bounty but are exposed to her furious moods. Such a culture venerates *The Venus of Willendorf*.

As humans gain control over nature, religions become Sky-Cults. Sky-cults have male Gods that design, instruct, order.

Sky-cults are found in civilizations with a much firmer grip over nature. Mother nature has been partially and temporarily subdued via human intelligence. Paglia argues that Judaism and Christianity are sky-cults—they worship an intelligent male God, not Mother nature.

Nefertiti is the artwork that would predictably emerge in a culture that is transitioning from an Earth-cult to a Sky-cult. Ancient Egypt was just such a culture. Paglia: "The pregnancy of Venus of Willendorf is displaced upward and redefined." The head is now *pregnant* with ideas.

Paglia: "Willendorf is chthonian belly-magic, Nefertiti Apollonian head-magic." By chthonian Paglia means the darkness and ignorance that hung over the primitive man. By Apollonian she means the light and clarity that civilization brought in via technical and social advancements.

If Willendorf is a fertility Goddess, Nefertiti is an intellect Goddess. Paglia writes that Nefertiti "seems futuristic" due to her enlarged skull. She strangely mirrors the aliens imagined in our science-fiction: both creatures have an overbearing brain.

Paglia writes: "Western culture, moving up toward Apollonian sunlight, discards one burden only to stagger under another." We use our brains to manage the moods, mystery, and challenges of nature—but an overdeveloped brain comes with its own moods, mystery, and challenges.

Paglia: " Mother nature is addition and multiplication, but Nefertiti is subtraction. Visually, she has been reduced to her essence." Nefertiti is a slick, minimalist cognitive machine; the "humpiness and horror of Mother earth," represented in Willendorf, is gone.

Paglia: "Venus of Willendorf is all body, Nefertiti all head." Paglia argues Nefertiti artistically foresaw "Greek categorical thought" and the "stringency, rigor, channeled ideas" of science. But heavy lies the crown: "Nefertiti's head is so massive it threatens to snap the neck."

10

DO YOU THINK LIKE A
HEDGEHOG OR A FOX?

The Hedgehog and the Fox, 1953

All generalizations are wrong but some are extraordinarily useful. One such generalization comes from Isaiah Berlin. Berlin writes that there are broadly two ways of thinking about the world—and investigates the special case of Leo Tolstoy who was unfortunately stranded in the middle. Dig in:

5th century B.C. Greek poet Archilochus wrote: "The fox knows many things, but the hedgehog knows one big thing." This is the seed from which Berlin's essay grows. In the jungle, the foxes hunt hedgehogs. Foxes are smarter, have more versatile strategies, but they're often beaten by the only move a hedgehog has: the spikes on its body.

Berlin takes this jungle scene to explain the two big thinking styles among humans. This contrast between the fox and the hedgehog sheds light on "the deepest differences which divide writers, thinkers, and human beings in general."

Hedgehogs are people with a "single central vision" from which they "understand, think and feel." Hedgehogs arrange what they know in holistic frameworks.

Foxes have no uniform "moral or aesthetic principle". They believe "no theories can possibly fit the immense variety of human behavior." The mind of a fox is scattered, and capable of pursuing many different ends that may be "unrelated and even contradictory."

For Berlin, Nietzsche, Plato, and Dostoevsky are some famous hedgehogs. They had a "fanatical inner vision." They connected different strands of knowledge with a thread that united them all. Their philosophy has a *panoramic* quality: wide and all-inclusive.

Berlin considers Herodotus, Aristotle, and Goethe to be foxes. Their vision of life was less panoramic and more kaleidoscopic. Foxes notice specific cases over general categories. For a fox life has a "vast multiplicity" that can't be reduced to a single principle.

Leo Tolstoy was an exceptional case. Berlin writes Tolstoy was a fox who desperately yearned to be a hedgehog. Tolstoy was hyper-sensitive to the minute details that compose life, and yet he wanted a universal story that connected it all.

Tolstoy the fox had "an incurable love of the concrete, the empirical, and the verifiable." He intuitively distrusted anything abstract, and mocked Napoleon in

War and Peace as Napoleon was a "master theorist" chasing a singular vision.

Tolstoy the hedgehog had a strong "desire to penetrate to first causes." He longed for "a universal explanatory principle" that made the chaos of life more coherent. But the gap between what he wanted and who he was, was too big to bridge.

Tolstoy's tragedy was that he "looked for a harmonious universe, but everywhere found war and disorder." Tolstoy was a "battering-ram" that attacked weak metaphysical structures, but his deepest spiritual need was to be stopped by an immovable obstacle. It was not to be.

Berlin describes Tolstoy as "a fox bitterly intent upon seeing like a hedgehog." Tolstoy was "by nature not a visionary." His ability to perceive differences, specificities, and idiosyncrasies left his desire for "a vision of the whole" unfulfilled.

11

DO YOU THINK LIKE A COMMISSAR OR A YOGI?

The Yogi and the Commissar, 1945

Arthur Koestler is among the 20th century's most famous ex-communists. He wrote bestselling novels and created right-wing propaganda to counter the rise of Communism. He also obsessively studied creativity for decades, producing books like *The Act of Creation* and *The Sleepwalkers: A History of Man's Changing Vision of the Universe.* **The Yogi and the Commissar** is Koestler's essay on two different thinking styles, and how world history swings from one to the other. Dig in:

The commissar is a person who wants to change the world outside. The "yogi" wants to transform the world inside.

The commissar sees the *tangible* world of goods, scarcity, and suffering. The yogi sees the *intangible* world of ethics, dreams, and spirits.

Means versus Ends. The commissar is comfortable using ignoble means—"violence, ruse, treachery and poison"—to achieve his noble ends. The yogi argues the opposite: the end is never known, and hence "means alone count."

Logic versus Vision. The commissar is a materialist, and considers the universe a "very large clockwork" knowable through logic. The yogi is an artist, and considers the universe a mystery *partially* knowable through visions.

The commissar addresses person-society relations while the yogi looks at person-universe relations.

The yogi and the commissar can strike a temporary accommodation, come to an uneasy compromise...but they can never reach a full synthesis. The schism remains.

Never go full commissar. Logic can lead to dark places. Consider this train of argument: A nation has a right to self defense—but the best defense is *attack*. Now add this: An "increase of ruthlessness shortens the struggle." Through coherent logic one has reached the doors of a war.

Never go full yogi. Putting principle above all can also lead to dark places. Against a remorseless tyrant, the principle of non-violence just translates to "passive submission to bayoneting and raping."

In the 19th century, physics saw the world as coherent and knowable. In the 20th century, quantum theory came in, "unmeasurable factors" were found, and metaphysics returned. Hence the development of physics shows the tension and interaction between the commissar and the yogi.

History as a pendulum. The world swings back and forth from the commissar to the yogi. In the 19th century, materialism, logic, and other commissar values were ascendant. In the 20th century, mass psychosis, the unconscious, and the yogi phase made a comeback.

An interesting question to ponder: Are we living today under the tyranny of commissars, or yogis?

12

9 WRITING TIPS FROM THE HIGHEST SELLING WRITING GUIDE

The Elements of Style, 1918

Napoleon Bonaparte once said the nobility could've kept their heads in the French Revolution if they'd mastered the writing desk. He meant they should have learnt to manipulate public perception via words. In the interest of keeping heads and influencing men when necessary, here are the best tips from *The Elements Of Style*. It's the highest selling writing guide of all time:

Make clear assertions: "Avoid tame, colorless, hesitating, non-committal language." Be direct, bold, and concise. Give the reader a shapely idea he can grip—not an amorphous blob that slips away from his hands.

Don't just negate—affirm: "Consciously or unconsciously, the reader is dissatisfied with being told only what is not; he wishes to be told what *is*." Strunk says it's "better to express a negative in a positive form." Example: Don't say "Not important"—say *trifling*.

Eliminate everything unnecessary: "A sentence should contain no unnecessary words, a paragraph no unnecessary sentences, for the same reason that a drawing should have no unnecessary lines and a machine no unnecessary parts."

Michelangelo: "Every block of stone has a statue inside it and it is the task of the sculptor to discover it."

Sentences with shared structures are rhythmic. Rhythmic sentences are easier to absorb and remember. William Strunk: "Express coordinate ideas in similar form." Similar form create rhythm, which makes your ideas *stickier*.

Imitation is impossible to avoid—the best we can do is imitate what is worth imitating: "Never imitate consciously, but do not worry about being an imitator; take pains instead to admire what is good."

Vagueness is evil and it poisons not just prose, but life too: "Death on the highway caused by a badly worded road sign, heartbreak among lovers caused by a misplaced phrase in a well-intentioned letter...Think of the tragedies that are rooted in ambiguity, and be clear!"

Space out your similes and metaphors: " Readers need time to catch their breath; they can't be expected to compare everything with something else, and no relief in sight. When you use metaphor, do not mix it up."

Where does style come from? From the soul of the writer: "Style is the writer, and therefore what you are, rather than what you know, will at last determine your style." Novel ideas come from novel experiences. Writing must pour forth from your life, not just your mind.

PART TWO

B FOR BALLS

13

ADVENTURE: A SPIRITUAL ANALYSIS

Twelve Against The Gods, 1929

When he gets some time off from snatching rockets midair, becoming the world's best Diablo player, and reshaping global politics, Elon Musk reads. Then he blasts out book recommendations. Usually he recommends classics I've read or at least heard of: *Hitchhikers' Guide To The Galaxy, The Story of Civilization, Storm of Steel, 1984, The Lord Of The Rings.* But in a 2016 interview with Bloomberg, he recommended a book I'd never seen in any library, bookstore, or blog: *12 Against The Gods* by Robert Bolitho (1929). So I read it. It's phenomenal. At its core, this book is a study of exceptional human beings. The subtitle—*The story of adventure*—refers not just to the specific adventures of the 12 people covered in the book (Napoleon, Alexander, Casanova among others), but to the *spiritual nature* of adventure itself. What mad *impulse* drives a select few to take on the world with nothing but their arrogance? What sorcery enables some men to live outside the rules of propriety, the limits of what's possible, and the guardrails set by the Gods themselves? Bolitho answers are poetic but strangely convincing.

Bolitho also raises, and answers, one more important question:

What is the true cost of greatness? (Spoiler: it's...high).

Bolitho starts off guns blazing in the introduction. He writes that laws are made for, and by, old men. Adventurers, on the other hand, are mavericks who treat laws with disdain. In fact, Bolitho writes, there's a certain "wickedness" inherent in the very concept of Adventure. Let's not tell white-washed tales about those who push the envelope—*real pioneers have something beastly in them.*

Bolitho writes that there's a spiritual divide inside man: "We, like the eagles, were born to be free. Yet we are obliged, in order to live at all, to make a cage of laws for ourselves and to stand on the perch. We are born as wasteful and unremorseful as tigers; we are obliged to be thrifty or starve, or freeze. We are born to wander, and cursed to stay and dig."

Greed powers the adventurer. He is egotistical, solitary, vain, and has a monstrous appetite for glory. Bolitho writes: "God help the ungreedy." The battle between the insatiable and the tranquil can have only one outcome...

Bolitho on why society needs the law breaker: "At the beginning of most careers stands an adventure, and so with states, institutions, civilizations. **The progress of humanity, whatever its mysterious direction, is not motored by mere momentum.** There is therefore a sociological role of adventure; necessarily an accidental one, since it is in itself non-social. **History is jolted along with great breaches of law and order, by adventurers and adventures.**"

The first adventurer annoyed everyone, subverted expectations, overstepped boundaries, sparked off disorder, and brought back unexpected gifts. Bolitho describes the love-hate relationship between adventurers and the rest of society: "The first adventurer was a nuisance; he left the tribal barricade open to risk...when he left to find out what made that noise in the night. I am sure he acted against his mother's, his wife's, and the council of old men's strict orders, when he did it. But it was he that found where the mammoths die and where after a thousand years of use there was still enough ivory to equip the whole tribe with weapons. **Such is the ultimate outline of the adventurer; Society's benefactor as well as pest.**"

Bolitho writes that the adventurer wages a two-front war against his society and against "the Unknown itself." However, the final tragedy is that even those who escape the clutches of society, and triumph over the great Unknown, *still* fall prey to one final villain: complacency. The successful adventurers end up acquiring so much that they stop to conserve. And that's when Fortune deserts them. Fortuna, the Goddess of Luck, loves the young, the wild, the restless—and detests the settled, the slow-footed, the calculating. Bolitho writes: "There is a more subtle tragedy that waits for adventurers than ruin, old age, rags, contempt. It is that he is doomed to cease to be an adventurer."

Bolitho has an unforgettable line about Alexander The Great: "Fire is a good word for Alexander, who lived like Fire, fought like Fire and died young, burnt out."

Alexander's father, Philip II of Macedon, cast a long shadow. He was an Olympic athlete, formidable military general, king of Macedonia, and "captain general" of all Greece. Young Alexander was always vexed, not thrilled, when he heard the news of his father's victories. He told his friends: "My father will go on conquering till there is nothing extraordinary left for you and me to do." Here's how Bolitho describes young Alexander's psychology: "For he did not desire to inherit a kingdom that would bring him opulence, luxury and pleasure, but one that would afford him wars, conflicts, and all the exercise of great ambition."

His father Phillip set the bar high—and then Alexander's mother, Olympias, told him something strange. She told him his *real* father wasn't Phillip, but Jupiter, a God in the Greek pantheon. This story got seared on young Alexander's impressionable mind. Olympias taught him to say: "I am a son of Earth and Heaven." Bolitho explains how Alexander's half-divine origin story became a useful fiction: "Believing he was a God, Alexander conquered the civilized world, and in the end was worshipped on his throne; if he had stayed at being a hero, he wouldn't have gone so far." It's *slightly* easier to perform inhuman feats of ingenuity and courage when you believe yourself to be half-God.

Alexander cultivated a contempt for bodily pleasures. In Bolitho's words, "the pleasures of bed and table" were "dangerous handicaps" to him. Delicious food and beautiful women were petty pleasures compared to Alexander's one true desire: a conquest of the whole world.

Bolitho talks about Alexander's "unification of will." He calls it Alexander's greatest advantage—one that is "unattainable" for most men. He was brilliant, brave, lucky, yes...but above all he was "purged of contradiction." To unify one's will has never been easy at any point in human history—but today it's harder than ever before. A dark cloud of skepticism hangs over everything that was previously sacred. Screens splay and splinter your attention. Notifications want to notify you. Stimulants want to stimulate you. Social media wants to drip feed you infinite entertainment. In such a world, he who can unify his will and focus it in one direction will have an almost insurmountable edge over the distracted masses.

Back to Alexander. His military track record was impeccable—he never lost a single battle. He defeated the Persian king Darius, who had the largest empire in the world. Alexander overcame fearsome odds in war—at one point beating a Persian army that was 5 times bigger. The night before a particularly onerous battle, his generals came to see him. They begged him to launch a surprise night attack—they said it was their only shot at winning. Alexander scoffed at the idea: "I will not steal a victory." (They won the next morning.) He set up Alexandria—which became the Ancient world's largest city. Alexander drove on, unstoppable, inexorable, reaching the far-flung plains of North India...until he suddenly died on his way back to Greece. He was 33. Malaria? Assassination? Historians debate to this day. Like a meteor he lit up human history and then disappeared in the dark. He left behind a legend that inspires men two thousand years later.

And legends matter more than you think—Bolitho writes that we spend all our life working out the implications of the legendary stories that catch our fancy in childhood. From *12 Against The Gods:* "The epic...has a great, though usually unsuspected, importance in most human lives. Most men, in the most inward explanation of the apparent diversity of their characteristics, in the terms of their own secret, are the hero of an unwritten book, a sequel to one they once read."

Bolitho on why we need art: "Life, that winged swift thing, has to be shot down and re-posed by art, like a stuffed bird, before we can use it as a model. There is, therefore, in religion and ethics always art; personality has to be simplified, wired; both its incidents and its results theorized and coordinated before it can awake that only instinct working to our own advantage with which we are endowed: imitation." Artists re-render the messy lives of heroes into simpler, imitable stories. A story can *inspire*—while a sprawling, objectively accurate biography can only *overwhelm*.

Normal people think the risk-takers are retarded. The non-adventurers believe the adventurers to be asinine. And, Bolitho admits, they're right: "The truly noble must have a dash of the idiotic in it to put it out of the reach of baseness, which is nothing but the commonest of common sense." But then Bolitho wonderfully flips the argument on its head. Considered more deeply, it is the normal man who is insane. The normal man "knowing the better follows the worse...refuses what he wants, and takes what disgusts him...sails his life against his compass, and yet stares and gasps at the lunacy of such rare persons who keep the course." Everyone enjoys superhero movies, everyone watches sports to soak in sublime athletic performances, everyone recalls the small heroisms of one's own life with great pride. And yet when it's time to chase a bigger heroism, to put on a sublime performance of one's *own*, to *live* a life that would make a great movie...we suddenly shrink. Only the adventurer follows through. He is the consistent one. It is the rest of us who are guilty of a maddening inconsistency: admiring what we dare not pursue.

There are countless other tidbits and stories in *Twelve Against The Gods*. I'll end with two:

A powerful quote from Cassanova on how stubbornness melts through everything: "I have always believed that when a man gets it into his head to do something, and when he exclusively occupies himself in that design, he must succeed whatever the difficulties. That man will become Grand Vizier or Pope. He will upset a dynasty, provided he starts young and has the brain and perseverance necessary..."

Talking of upsetting dynasties, here's a fascinating report from a French military school describing Napoleon at 15: "Reserved and diligent, he prefers study to any kind of conversation, and nourishes his mind on good authors. He is taciturn, with a love of solitude; is moody, overbearing and extremely egotistical. Though he speaks little, his answers are decisive and to the point, and he excels in argument. Much self-love and overweening ambition..."

14

HOW TO BECOME A MAN OF HISTORY

On the Use and Abuse of History for Life, 1874

What does it take to become a man of history? Nietzsche answers this question in a 150 year old essay. He shows how the wrong relationship with history will cripple you. But the right relationship will shake off your timid lethargy and birth within you an unquenchable lust for greatness.

I think it's the greatest essay ever written. It's top insights:

History paralyzes you. History says: build a company and it'll fall. Write a book and people will forget. Create a new empire and it'll decline. History is a story of endings. It freezes us into inaction—a man with total historical awareness cannot "dare" raise a "finger."

Nietzsche wrote that the typical reader of history is an "idler in the garden of knowledge." But Nietzsche's relationship with history is different: "We need history for the sake of life and action, not so as to turn comfortably away from life and action." Nietzsche: "We want to serve history only to the extent that history serves life." What is the point of accumulating knowledge if life itself becomes "stunted and degenerate" in the process?

Nietzsche draws a link between growth and having no past. Children have nothing to look back on, they live *ahistorically*, and are more capable of growth than humans at any other time in their life. Nietzsche writes this forgetfulness is a "vital foundation" for health. Forgetting the past is as necessary to human health as forgetting consciousness during sleep. Nietzsche: "Forgetting is essential to action of any kind, just as not only light but darkness too is essential for the life of everything organic."

Who does history BELONG to? To ambitious souls seeking greatness. Nietzsche: "History belongs above all to the man of deeds and power, to him who fights a great fight, who needs models, teachers, comforters and cannot find them among his contemporaries."

Nietzsche wrote that masses can only ever do one of three things: "The masses seem to me to deserve notice in 3 respects only: first as faded copies of great men produced on poor paper with worn-out plates, then as a force of resistance to great men, finally as instruments in the hands of great men." Aspiring men of history will have to utilize the masses to actualize their vision, so it's important to understand their core nature.

Nietzsche on how greatness always finds resistance: "All that is base and petty, filling every corner of the earth, casts itself across the path that greatness has to tread on its way to immortality and retards, deceives, and suffocates it." Expect sabotage from normies.

But this sabotage must be overcome, not to stroke our ego, but to enter the most sacred *brotherhood* there is. Nietzsche wrote that history is a "relay race" where the torch of excellence is passed on from the greats of one generation to the greats of the next. Grab the torch and run.

Nietzsche's fiery career advice: Do work that contains the "monogram" of your "most essential being." A monogram is a signature. When you sew your initials into a handkerchief so it would be recognizably yours, you make a monogram. Nietzsche's advice is to cultivate a unique signature and stamp it on everything you do. Men of history are often known by their distinct style. A way of being that is unmistakably theirs.

The modern man is a house divided against itself. Nietzsche said that inside modern people, there's a "remarkable antithesis between an interior which fails to correspond to any exterior and an exterior which fails to correspond to any interior." We act out what we do not believe and we believe what we dare not voice. Lesson: Only strong people make history. Only internally coherent people can be strong. Stop being a house divided against itself, and set up your life on a firm foundation.

Only by trying to be great yourself will you begin to understand the greatness of the past. Nietzsche: "Only when you put forth your noblest qualities in all their strength will you divine what is worth knowing and preserving in the past. Like to like!" You cannot extract anything valuable from history by mastering mere information about it. You can only meaningfully borrow from history by embodying the energy and attitude of the men who shaped it. Nietzsche's full quote continues to haunt me: "He who has not experienced greater and more exalted things than others won't know how to interpret the great and exalted things of the past. When the past speaks it always speaks as an oracle: only if you are an architect of the future and know the present will you understand it." Takeaway: the more you strive to shape the future, the louder the past clamors to teach you lessons. But if you become passive as a plant, the past will become perfectly mute.

15

WE WANT TO EXALT
AGGRESSION

The Futurist Manifesto, 1909

Filippo Tommaso Marinetti was an Italian poet. At age 33, in the year 1909, he was in a late night car accident. He survived it. Riding a wave of excitement, stress, and adrenaline, he wrote up the Futurist Manifesto the same night. It's 4 pages of glorious, red-blooded prose. It has been credited and/or blamed for the rise of Fascism. In the 115 years then, it has lost none of its freshness, energy, and shock value. Strap in:

The futurist manifesto is above all a "testament to all the living men on earth."

Futurists are men in revolt against the world, and they are proud to stand alone. Marinetti: "Our hearts were filled with an immense pride at feeling ourselves standing quite alone, like lighthouses or like the sentinels in an outpost."

The future will be made by men willing to "leave good sense behind like a hideous husk."

Marinetti notes three essential elements of all futurist art: "courage, audacity and revolt." The futurists are against "all opportunist and utilitarian cowardice." They seek not security but adventure.

Futurist literature must be a *monument* to energetic activity: "Literature has up to now magnified pensive immobility and slumber. We want to exalt movements of aggression, feverish sleeplessness, the perilous leap, the slap and the blow with the fist."

The need for speed: "The world has been enriched by a new beauty: the beauty of speed." Marinetti writes: "Our hearts are not in the least tired. For they are nourished by fire, hatred and speed! Does this surprise you? It is because you do not even remember being alive!" To be truly alive is to sometimes find nourishment—in hate.

Artists must not hold themselves back. They must burn and blaze like candles lit from both ends. Marinetti: "The poet must spend himself with warmth, glamor and prodigality."

Conquest is the most aesthetic thing in the world. My favorite lines from the Futurist Manifesto: "Beauty exists only in struggle. There is no masterpiece that has not an aggressive character. Poetry must be a violent assault on the forces of the unknown, to force them to bow before man."

Marinetti's ferocious critique of museums is worth noting, even though I disagree with it: "Museums, cemeteries! Truly identical in their sinister juxtaposition of bodies that do not know each other. Public dormitories where you sleep side by side for ever with beings you hate or do not know." *Phew.* A counterpoint, if I may: Greatness and beauty exist outside of time, and the grandeur of the past very much still speaks to us. Marinetti's manifesto, now 115 years old, is a good case in point.

Cultivate a "proud indefatigable courage." The jungle is starved for lions.

16

THE NERD-JOCK DICHOTOMY IS FALSE

A life of action does not mean you have to be an intellectual dunce, and reading books does not mean you need to check out of life. Let me show you 10 writers who lived like action heroes.

Ernst Jünger fought WW-I at 19, saw intense action at the frontlines, led his unit to impossible victories, was wounded 7 times, survived headshots, read Nietzsche in his spare time, and self-published the war classic *Storm Of Steel* in 1920.

Lawrence Of Arabia cycled 3,500 km+ and walked 1,600+ km to study castles at the age of 19, became one of the Allied leaders of the Arab Revolt during WW1, became a seaplane expert, wrote the best-selling *Seven Pillars Of Wisdom*, and died in a mysterious bike crash at 46.

Julius Caesar. Perhaps the greatest king in history, his very name became synonymous with absolute authority: Caesar, Kaiser, Tzar. He wrote many poems and tragedies that don't survive. His books on the Gaul campaigns and the Civil War do, and have a unique muscular style.

Roald Dahl shot down more than five enemy planes in WWII, climbed out of the wreckage of a burning plane, went blind, recovered his vision, became a spy, seduced famous women to gather intelligence secrets, wrote Matilda and other classics, and became the highest earning dead man of 2021 due to Netflix adapting his books.

Charles Lindbergh was the first man ever to fly nonstop from NYC to Paris, caused the global Aviation boom, was *Time's* first ever **Man Of The Year**, invented the perfusion pump which makes organ transplants possible today, and wrote "We"—one of the best-sellers of 1927.

Socrates fought at least 3 major battles in the Peloponnesian War, notably protected two of his fellow soldiers from the enemy when they were injured, fought till he was 50 years with men half his age, advised generals, and became the most famous philosopher in history.

Wittgenstein was one of the richest men in the world in 1914 and qualified for a medical exemption in WWI. He went to the frontlines anyway, always took the most dangerous positions, won the highest honors, and became one of the most influential thinkers of the century.

Aeschylus invented the very genre of tragedy and won multiple awards at Dionysia—the Intellectual Olympics of Ancient Athens. And yet he was so much prouder of his military victories that on his tombstone, only his war career is mentioned.

André Malraux rediscovered lost cities, launched archeological expeditions for exotic temples, became a P.O.W. in WWII, got freed and led a brigade, and became France's first Culture Minister under De Gaulle. His novel "Man's Fate" won France's highest literary award.

Dennis Wheatley was expelled from college, fell prey to chemical warfare in WWI, and saw his wine business shut down in the Great Depression. But then he became the world's best-selling author and a pivotal member of the British Information Warfare team in WWII.

17

WHEN VICES LOOK LIKE VIRTUES

Moral Maxims and Reflections, 1665

La Rochefoucauld fought wars, wrote aphorisms denser than most books, and was among the preeminent noblemen of 17th century France. He left a lasting impact on Nietzsche. Discover 14 great aphorisms from Rochefoucauld:

Lethargy and cowardice are vices that know how to look like virtues: "We are held to our duty by laziness and timidity, but often our virtue gets all the credit." Some people rebrand their inertia as consistency. Others rebrand their cowardice as a stoic control over emotions.

Charisma is being comfortable in your own skin. Here's Rochefoucauld on how to be irresistible: "There is an air which belongs to the figure and talents of each individual...We should try to find out what air is natural to us and never abandon it, but make it as perfect as we can." Authenticity is hot.

Self-constraint is only a virtue when your unconstrained self is capable of causing damage: "Nobody deserves to be praised for goodness unless he is strong enough to be bad, for any other goodness is usually merely inertia or lack of will-power." Only the monster can be nice.

Another vice that gets more of a pass than it should? Laziness: "Of all our faults we think most leniently of laziness; we deceive ourselves into believing that...instead of destroying our other qualities, it merely suspends their functions."

What does love need to survive? Movement: "Neither love nor fire can subsist without perpetual motion; both cease to live so soon as they cease to hope, or to fear." Love is sustained by the fear of its loss, and the expectation of interesting tomorrows to be spent together.

Sometimes, a lack of any serious flaw just means you've led a lukewarm, uneventful life: "Some people are so shallow and frivolous that they are as far removed from having any real faults as from having any solid virtues."

Not all the good things about you will be seen and appreciated. If a person fails to notice and value a certain virtue of yours, it may be because he lacks the "sense" for it: "Certain good qualities are like the senses; those who lack them can neither appreciate nor understand them."

Every single aspect of your personality can be used to your advantage: "There are foolish people who recognize their foolishness and use it skillfully."

Beware the hand of good old self-interest in everything: "Self-interest speaks all kinds of languages and plays all kinds of parts--even that of disinterestedness. "

Halfway trust is unsatisfying for both parties: "We should make it a rule never to have half confidences. They always embarrass those who give them, and dissatisfy those who receive them. It is far safer and more honest to tell nothing than to be silent when we have begun to tell."

Against hyperbole: "Never let the words be grander than the matter."

Don't let trivial concerns steal all your energy, time, and will-power: "People too much taken up with little things usually become incapable of big ones."

Distance is the acid test for love. La Rochefoucauld: "Absence diminishes small loves and increases great ones, as the wind blows out the candle and fans the bonfire." Time and distance only ever take away everything superfluous while deepening everything real.

Thinkers versus Doers: "Thinkers think and doers do. But until the thinkers do and the doers think, progress will be just another word."

18

HOW HATE IS A MUSE

Zen In The Art Of Writing, 1990

You know Ray Bradbury's classic dystopian novel, *Fahrenheit 451*. Christian Bale acted in the 2002 movie adaptation, *Equilibrium*. Ray Bradbury was a born storyteller—he made his first dollar selling a joke to a radio show at 14. Bradbury wrote a guide for creative people, and one of its great counter-intuitive insights is that hate can be a muse.

Dig in:

Good ideas are like hot women. Chasing them will only scare them "off into the woods." Ray Bradbury's advice: Whistle, "saunter along," and cultivate a "carefully acquired disdain." The muse is attracted to a confident indifference.

Creativity can come from hate too. Anything that incites emotions in you—including your prejudices—will make for interesting writing. Ray Bradbury asks: "When was the last time you dared release a cherished prejudice so it slammed the page like a lightning bolt?" Even if your readers disagree with you, they will still appreciate the force and sincerity of your convictions.

Another great question from Bradbury: "What are the best things and the worst things in your life, and when are you going to get around to whispering or shouting them?"

Great art is impossible without enthusiasm. Ray Bradbury: "Everything I've ever done was done with excitement, because I wanted to do it, because I loved doing it." Do things that spark off a certain "fever, ardor, and delight" in you. And you'll do them *artistically.*

Bradbury once wrote a story out of "pure indignation." His night walks were interrupted so often by the police that he wrote *The Pedestrian*: "A story of a time when a man is arrested and taken off for clinical study because he insists on looking at un-televised reality." Modern culture is over-indexed on compassion. We ignore or castrate inconvenient feelings of indignation, disgust, and hate...but they can be rife with creative possibilities.

The most important things about a writer are his "zests, appetites, and hungers." All the greatest books are "bursting with animal vigor and intellectual vitality." Bradbury: " Think of Shakespeare and Melville and you think of thunder, lightning, and wind." People today are working from the incorrect assumption that dry ideas are the only things worth communicating. But Bradbury is arguing that the texture of your life, the *spirit* of your *being,* is infinitely more worthy of being passed on than your "ideas" per say. And this spirit lives in your zests, appetites, and hungers.

A final word from Bradbury: "The first thing a writer should be is—excited. He should be a thing of fevers and enthusiasms. Without such vigor, he might as well be out picking peaches or digging ditches; God knows it'd be better for his health."

19

HOW VAGUE WORDS MAKE YOU WEAK

The Spirit of Romance, 1910

ABC of Reading, 1934

Ezra Pound was a pioneering poet who inspired everyone from Hemingway to T.S. Eliot. He was also a Mussolini Superfan. After the axis powers lost the war, Pound was declared mad in 1945 and institutionalized for 12 years. But no matter how "problematic" his politics, Pound was a brilliant artist full of valuable insights on how to design your reading list, why civilizations die, and how vague words make humans weak. Dig in.

Pound on how to design your reading list: "Properly, we should read for power. Man reading should be man intensely alive. The book should be a ball of light in one's hand." We read for entertainment, distraction, solace—but why not read for power?

Rome fell as its language fell. Pound: "Rome rose with the idiom of Caesar, Ovid, and Tacitus, she declined in a welter of rhetoric, the diplomat's language to conceal thought...Rome went because it was no longer the fashion to hit the nail on the head. They desired orators."

Pound on how to lose an empire: "A people that grows accustomed to sloppy writing is a people in process of losing grip on its empire and on itself." Vague words betray a mind that is afraid of conclusions. You lose power over reality by first losing your *conceptual* grip.

Pound on putting your skin in the game: "If a man isn't willing to take some risk for his opinions, either his opinions are no good or he's no good." In the preface to Guide To Kulchur, Pound notes that he will be committing himself to ideas that "very few men can *afford* to."

Pound on why literature is hero-worship: "The history of an art is the history of masterwork, not of failures, or mediocrity. The omniscient historian would display the masterpieces, their causes and their inter-relation. The study of literature is hero-worship."

The greatest of art foists "sudden growth" upon us. It helps us grasp a complicated emotion or idea in a flash via the means of an elegant "image." The sensation of "sudden liberation" that accompanies great art derives precisely from this image.

Pound against relativism: "When words cease to cling close to things, kingdoms fall, empires wane and diminish." GK Chesterton agrees: "Fires will be kindled to testify that two and two make four. Swords will be drawn to prove that leaves are green in summer." Pound wrote that when language becomes "slushy and inexact, or excessive or bloated," then the "whole machinery of social and of individual thought and order goes to pot."

The job of an artist is to help his audience "escape from dullness." What a good writer must do: "relieve, refresh, revive the mind of the reader—with some form of ecstasy, by some splendor of thought, some presentation of sheer beauty, some lightning turn of phrase." If your prose can make people's blood flow faster, they'll remember your ideas.

Pound on the right way to study literature: "The proper METHOD for studying poetry and good letters is the method of contemporary biologists, that is careful first-hand examination of the matter, and continual *comparison* of one slide or specimen with another." People today are scared to compare because that means inevitably putting one thing above another. But only he who is willing to compare, contrast, and judge can discover meaningful truths.

Ezra Pound defines great literature: "Great literature is simply language charged with meaning to the utmost possible degree." Bad writing is when the words are weak, the sentences meandering, and the paragraphs unsure of their own conclusion.

20

IN DEFENSE OF STRONG FEELINGS

A Defense of Enthusiasm, 1835

Henry Tuckerman was a 19th century critic who saw that people were losing their enthusiasm for life. The bane of modern man is too much thought and too little action. Strong feelings, for all their faults that the stoics never fail to mention, are actually a way out of this conundrum. They *jolt* people enough to act.

Henry Tuckerman: "While the mere intellectual man speculates...the man of feeling acts, realizes, puts forth his complete energies. His earnest and strong heart will not let his mind rest; he is urged by an inward impulse to *embody* his thought." Dear overthinker, embody your thought.

Henry Tuckerman wrote that stuffing your brain with information that evokes no emotion—and inspires no action—is to gain knowledge "at the expense of the soul." You become a "pedant and logician" who's dead inside.

What's better than intelligence? A sensitivity for beauty, and a bias for action: "That quickness of apprehension which New Englanders call smartness, is not so valuable as sensibility to the beautiful...and the world of action and feeling."

Passion will highlight parts of reality that were invisible before. Tuckerman: "When the sentiments are interested, new facts spring to light." The *passionate* ones can see, think, and do what the merely *curious* can't.

The intellect "may illumine, but it cannot inspire." The intellect is akin to *moonlight*: "It may shed a cold radiance upon the path of life, but it warms no flower into bloom; it sets free no icebound fountains. " Emotions are akin to *sunlight*: they make *growth* possible. The power of reason is like the light of the moon—it makes you see a little better but that's about it. The power of feelings is like sunlight—it is the blaze by which life itself grows.

Tuckerman on how enthusiasm fuels great art: "Ponder the lives of the glorious in art or literature through all the ages. What are they but records of toils and sacrifices supported by earnest hearts?" The big mistake of contemporary schooling is focussing on critical thinking while totally ignoring *earnest feeling.* A great system for developing lop-sided humans.

While reason may show us the path to our goal, it's feelings that give us the energy to walk the path. Our emotions and feelings, despite their inherent messiness, are worth holding onto.

Life can't ever be made "mechanical." Tuckerman: "Life is encircled by mystery, brightened by affection, and solemnized by death." It is the non-mechanical aspects of life that give it meaning.

We can't avoid "visions of glory and dreams of love and hopes of heaven." Hold on to your visions, dreams, and hopes—no matter how unreasonable.

The "empire of utility" is a small one; a wider universe exists outside it. It is yours for the taking, if you can let go of reason.

21

WHEN HIGH IQ BECOMES A PROBLEM

British novelist John Fowles explains in **The Aristos** (1964) how high IQ can subvert your will to act: "High intelligence leads to multiplicity of interest and a sharpened capacity to foresee the consequences of any action. Will is lost in a labyrinth of hypothesis." Rule 1: Do not lose the will.

The Aristos: "Throughout history the intelligentsia have been despised for their weakness as enactors."

Thomas Carlyle, remembered for his "Great Man Theory" of history, wrote in 1841: "A man lives by believing something; not by debating and arguing about many things." Life is empty without action, action is impossible if you are too busy arguing over intellectual minutiae.

G.K. Chesterton on how an open mind is no more a virtue than an open mouth: "The object of opening the mind, as of opening the mouth, is to shut it again on something solid." A mind that never closes is as tragic as a mind that never opens.

A knight who owns a sharp sword should make sure he does not cut himself with it, and a man gifted with a great mind should make sure he does not start living inside it.

Napoleon said the ideal combination is to be hyper-rational and paranoid before the battle...and then during the fight, to abandon yourself to destiny. My twitter friend *Stoop to Rise*(@StoopToRise) quotes Gracian: "Mediocrity obtains more with application than superiority without it."

Nietzsche says you sometimes need a "Will To Stupidity" as it helps you finish what you start. Knowledge eats itself but wisdom knows when to self-limit. Some solutions demand not strategy, cognition, or high-level abstraction, but a stupid stubbornness.

Ultimately we must love the rough but real labor of our hands more than we love the seductive designs of our imagination.

My twitter friend @AFreeLlama: "The trick is to know and serve your values. Understand that all choices have unforeseen consequences. Perfectionism is procrastination masquerading as quality control."

Life does not exist to serve the brain, the brain exists to serve Life.

22

THE STRANGE ADVANTAGES OF SHOOTING YOUR OWN LEG

The Handicap Principle, 1997

Why do men throw their money at diamond rings? Why do prey *reveal* themselves to nearby *predators*? The Handicap Principle, proposed in 1975 by Israeli biologist Amotz Zahavi, is why. He explained the principle in great detail in a 1997 book. Here are the book's core ideas:

Animals often do things that seem to go against their self-interest. Blabbers reveal their positions to their predators, gazelles waste precious time and energy by jumping up and down *after* getting spotted by predators, and crabs build sand castles right where waves destroy them.

What explains such irrationality or inefficiency? Some argue this is incomplete evolution, but Zahabi gives a different answer. These animals are not hurting themselves—to the contrary, they're signaling their strength and confidence.

By revealing their position, blabbers are telling the nearby raptor, its predator, that it has "no chance of catching them." By exposing itself and wasting energy, the gazelle signals: "I'm so fast I can handicap myself like this. So don't bother."

The crab signals: I'm so energetic and healthy I can afford to "continually rebuild" my sand castles. While blabbers and gazelles are signaling to rivals, the crab is signaling to potential mates. Animals, including humans, handicap themselves both in front of rivals and mates.

Here's something wild: Pelicans "grow fleshy bumps between their eyes" when looking to mate. This hurts their vision and damages their ability to look for fish. The signal is: "I'm such a *fishing* expert I can feed myself even with this handicap."

Zahavi gives another example: "Frog-eating bats locate their prey by their courtship calls." So what do the confident male frogs do? They croak *louder* than they need to. Zahavi: "Only a male frog that can successfully avoid bats despite disclosing its location to them can afford to croak much." The female frogs think: that's a ballsy guy, I'll go with him.

Humans handicap themselves to potential rivals and lovers too. Men often walk towards a rival, hands down and chin exposed. This threat works because the signal is: "I'm so strong I can bring my exposed face to you, thereby handicapping myself, and you still can't do a thing."

When looking to propose, men handicap their bank account with a diamond ring. The signals are: I'm resourceful—could a poor man do this? I'm trustworthy—could I do this with "many females simultaneously"? I'm sincere—would I put so much money on the line if I wasn't?

Some men are terribly arrogant. Why? Zahavi would argue they're putting the handicap principle to use. Arrogance exposes you to greater scrutiny and attack. Humility is safer, it's the "stay hidden" option. Arrogance is a self-inflicted handicap meant to demonstrate that you're so strong that you can "afford" it.

Animal behaviors that look stupid, inefficient, or merely decorative are actually better explained through the handicap principle. By handicapping oneself, an animal sends a reliable signal about its abundant power, strength, and sincerity.

23

WHY HEROES MATTER

André Malraux is a case study in greatness. He swept the biggest literary awards of his day, became a decorated war hero, and led an architectural restoration drive that made France the world's most touristed country. He was nominated for the Nobel Prize In Literature 32 times and became the world's first "culture minister." What made him tick? His life shows why intellectual men should prioritize action—and how having heroes is the ultimate performance enhancing drug.

Andre Malraux's wife wrote that her very first conversations with him were about " Novalis, Nietzsche, Dostoevsky." Malraux was particularly "haunted" by Nietzsche and aspired to the Nietzschean ideal of a thoughtful, risk-taking man of action.

Malraux's first published article—"The Origins of Cubist Poetry"—came out when he was 19. His surrealist short stories were well-received. He was becoming popular among the literary salons of Paris. But he suddenly packed bags and took his young wife to the Far East. Why?

Because of his second idol: T.E. Lawrence, better known as the Lawrence of Arabia. Lawrence was 13 years older and blazed a life path that left young Malraux in awe.

Malraux left a promising literary future in Paris and became an adventurer to follow in Lawrence's footsteps.

Lawrence had cycled alone for three thousand kilometers to research castles when he was just 20. Malraux, a decade later, trekked through dense Cambodian forests to find remains of abandoned temples. He was 21.

Malraux chanced upon the Banteay Srei temple in Cambodia—a thousand year old monument. He made away with 4 beautiful statues, intending to sell them to French museums, and was arrested by the French government for it.

Soon after, Malraux flew over the deserts of Saudi Arabia and Yemen in aircrafts—flying was barely a 20 year old technology at this point—right as the Saudi-Yemeni war raged on. He claimed to have found the mythical lost capital of Queen Sheba mentioned in the Old Testament.

In 1933, Malraux wrote in a novel: "Every man dreams of being God." Nietzsche would say: *No nobler dream.* (The novel won France's highest literary award, Prix Goncourt.)

T.E. Lawrence volunteered in World War 1, Malraux in World War II. Both came back decorated war heroes. Both talked about war as a spiritual exercise in pushing past one's limits and emerging from it renewed...almost baptized.

Malraux was captured by the Nazis in World War II. He escaped, organized a thousand men into an independent brigade, and liberated towns on the East of France.

Malraux was made the world's first "culture minister" by Charles De Gaulle. Malraux cleaned up the soot-ridden French architecture; today France is the most visited country in the world.

Malraux on the value of ACTION: "Often the difference between a successful person and a failure is not one has better abilities or ideas, but the courage that one has to bet on one's ideas, to take a calculated risk—and to act." Bet on your ideas. Take calculated risks. Act.

24

GREAT MEN ARE OFTEN BORED MEN

Memoirs from Beyond the Grave, 1848

Chateaubriand belonged to a French aristocratic family, almost died defending the Monarchy in the French revolution, and was embraced by Napoleon only to be exiled. His books were so influential that a young Victor Hugo said: "I will be Chateaubriand or nothing." What made him great?

Despite fighting wars, living through revolutions, and making friends and enemies among powerful Emperors, Chateaubriand was haunted by boredom all his life. To a friend he wrote: "I began to be bored in my mother's womb, and since then I have never been anything but bored."

Nothing seemed to excite Chateaubriand: "Everything wearies me: I haul my boredom through my days like a chain, and everywhere I go I yawn away my life." He got bored even while retelling his eventful stories: "The sound of my voice becomes intolerable to me; I hold my tongue."

Boredom pushed him to the ends of the Earth for adventure: "After suffering poverty, hunger, thirst, and exile, I have sat, a minister and ambassador, covered with gold lace, gaudy with ribbons and decorations, at the table of kings, the feasts of princes and princesses."

Discontentment is a gift. It makes you do more. Chateaubriand: "I have viewed closely the rarest disasters, the greatest good fortune, the highest reputations. I have been present at sieges, conclaves, at the restoration and demolition of thrones. I have made history, and been able to write it."

Boredom is good because it pushes you away from the trivial towards more eventful pastures. But it's important to not let the gift of boredom become the curse of a jumpy mind. Repeated *action* is often needed to turn a rough stone into a sleek work of art. Chateaubriand knew this: "I have never abandoned any project worth the trouble of completing."

Chateaubriand had the Talented Generalist's Curse—he had a "natural aptitude for almost everything." He liked "amusing things as well as serious ones." Here's how he managed to get things done despite his wide-ranging interests: "Even when I grow weary of my object, my persistence is always greater than my boredom."

Chateaubriand called himself a "bizarre androgyne forged by the divergent bloods of my mother and my father." He was simultaneously a "man of dreams" and a "man of realities." He was "passionate yet methodical"—a thoughtful writer living an action hero's life.

Chateaubriand on his friend Joubert: "He had adopted an idea of perfection that prevented him from finishing anything." Joubert himself wrote: "I am like an Aeolian harp that makes beautiful sounds and plays no tune." Chateaubriand thus understood that perfectionism was paralysis.

Chateaubriand on how to live masterfully: "A master in the art of living draws no sharp distinction between his work and his play; his labor and his leisure; his mind and his body; his education and his recreation. He hardly knows which is which."

Pursue only your "vision of excellence."

Chateaubriand believed too much peace makes a nation convenient prey for others: "I have spoken of the danger of war, but I must also recall the dangers of prolonged peace. If hostilities descend on an unwarlike people, would they be able to resist?"

Only the genuine threat of external attacks keeps a nation alert enough for liberty: "What best suits the complexion of a free society is a state of peace tempered by war or a state of war tempered by peace." Otherwise people get swamped by the "gentler habits of life."

With his novella *René*, Chateaubriand launched the romantic movement in France. His protagonist: "The ancient world had no certainty, the modern world had no beauty." In his Memoirs, Chateaubriand would write: "Beauty, a serious trifle, remains when all else has passed away."

Boredom often becomes bitterness. Chateaubriand knew this, and *consciously* avoided the sad fate of a cynic: "One is not superior merely because one sees the world as odious." He bled for his principles, created enduring works of art, and became a model for Thoughtful Adventurers of the future.

25

THE PRIMARY TRAIT OF A HERO

On Heroes, Hero-Worship, & the Heroic in History, 1841

Thomas Carlyle: "The History of the world is but the Biography of great men." But what are these great men like? Carlyle's answer: they are smart, they're self-aware, but above all they're sincere. Dig in.

First, the great men of history are intelligent generalists: "I have no notion of a truly great man that could not be all sorts of men. The Poet who could merely sit on a chair, and compose stanzas, would never make a stanza worth much. He couldn't sing the Heroic warrior unless he himself were a Heroic warrior too."

Second, Carlyle's hero is self-aware. He knows "by instinct" the following things: "What condition he works under, what his materials are, what his own force and its relation to them is." He accepts reality even when it's "feeble, forlorn."

But above all, great men are sincere. Carlyle emphasizes the hero's "ineradicable feeling for reality." While others make their peace with convenient lies and official make-believe, a hero can't help but remain truthful to reality as he sees it. His refusal to lie makes him fit to lead.

There's a lot in the world that is "regular, decorous, and accredited by...conclaves" that is nevertheless untrue. Heroes can't abide by views or decisions just because they are common, socially acceptable, or have the experts' approval. They want to discover, live by, and if necessary die by, the truth.

Carlyle writes that while most people can "walk in a vain show," heroes cannot. Heroes cannot live except in the "awful presence of Reality." Heroes refuse to lie for social credit points.

Carlyle writes that "the heart remains cold before" stately and dignified men who talk in "measured euphemisms." They don't inspire, they lack a hero's sincerity and passion. They manage the perceptions about reality; they don't master reality itself.

Unheroic individuals "fall into skepticism, dilettantism, and insincerity." Skeptics replace action with endless questioning, dilettantes replace commitment with permanent dabbling, and insincere people hide cowardice behind an ironic pose.

An aspiring hero must "stand upon things, and not shows of things." The hero respects his time and energy by not expending them upon illusions. His sincerity is the source of his greatness. His unrelenting grip on reality is why his actions have weight.

26

JOE ROGAN'S FAVORITE BOOK

The Book of Five Rings, 1645

Miyamoto Musashi, a Japanese samurai, holds the all-time record for dueling: undefeated across 61 fights. In Japan he's considered a "sword-saint." He wrote a book to explain his martial arts philosophy: *The Book of Five Rings* (1645). It's among Joe Rogan's favorite books. He calls it "one of the most valuable things anyone has ever written." Beyond martial arts, it's full of timeless life advice. Dig in:

Have no favorite weapon. Musashi cautions fighters against over-reliance on one move or "special fondness for a particular weapon". He writes: "Too much is the same as not enough." Stay pragmatic, don't entertain "likes and dislikes," and arm yourself with what you need for victory.

The rhythm matters. Everything around us is rhythmical: the seasons, music, dance, rising and falling fortunes—and martial arts. To win, predict and disrupt the enemy's rhythm. An enemy without his rhythm has no orientation and becomes a soft target.

Perception versus Observation. Perception is skimming the surface; observation is penetrating the depths. Musashi recommends detachment to what is close, and awareness of what is distant. He writes: "See that which is far away closely and what is nearby from a distance."

Become the opponent. What is your enemy's P.O.V.? This is not for compassion but for better gauging their self-perceived weaknesses. Step into the enemy's mind to see where the fear is—then strike there.

Moving shadows. Not able to look into the enemy's mind? Move shadows. "Pretend to make a powerful attack" and observe the reaction. The enemy will show his hand. Once their strategy is known, their defeat is imminent.

Remain mysterious: "Do not let the enemy see your spirit."

Become new. When "snarled up and making no progress," hit restart. Musashi uses a wonderful phrase: "toss your mood away." In a defeated mood, losses pile up. We can't travel back in time, but by going back to the *square one mentality*, we can overturn the negative momentum.

Bigger isn't always better. Musashi notes some fighters prefer long swords for their greater reach. But what if it becomes a close-quartered fight? Then a long sword can't swing back and forth like a shorter one can. Strength and power can't simply be pinned down to size.

Takeaways: Make false moves to force the enemy into revealing their hands. If you can peek into their mind, you can stab their heart. Avoid over-reliance on one move or weapon, and reverse negative momentum by mentally starting anew.

27

INSIDE NAPOLEON'S MIND

Thoughts by Napoléon Bonaparte, 1838

Napoleon in his own Words, 1916

Mind of Napoleon, 1915

Napoleon rescued France from revolutionary chaos, made it Europe's preeminent great power, and stacked up a military record better than Julius Caesar and Alexander the Great. He was moody, courageous, energetic, and brilliant beyond measure. Fortunately, we can peek into his mind via his own statements. Napoleon's words were recorded in his private letters, his speeches, his secretaries' memoirs, and thousands of newspaper reports. Here is a curation of 33 insights from the Emperor...

On freedom: "If one analyzes it, political freedom is an accepted myth thought up by those governing to put the governed to sleep." Power is always concentrated at the top—different political systems and doctrines are merely different ways of hiding this fact.

Napoleon on equality: "Equality exists only in theory." No man-made political programs can reverse the innate inequality of nature: "Social law can give all men equal rights. Nature will never give them equal faculties."

For Napoleon, Monarchies are more just than Democracies: "In the system of absolute power only one voice is necessary to rectify an injustice; in the assembly system five hundred are necessary."

Napoleon on being too cautious: "The torment of precaution is worse than the dangers it seeks to avoid: it is better to abandon yourself to destiny." The compulsive need to preempt and predict all problems is its own type of hell.

Napoleon on revolutions :"There are inevitable revolutions. They are moral eruptions, like the physical eruption of volcanoes. When the chemical combinations that produce the latter are complete, they explode, just like revolutions do when the moral combinations are in place." Here's another one: "A revolution is an opinion which discovers bayonets." With brevity, Napoleon combines the two poles of revolution: the ideas that set it off, and the material might that carries it to fruition.

A leader cannot fight the dominant ideas of his time: "Lead the ideas of your time and they will accompany and support you; fall behind them and they drag you along with them; oppose them and they will overwhelm you."

Napoleon on how politics is a young man's game: "In politics, young people are worth more than old people." Politics requires not just numbers, but loyal soldiers and energetic executioners of different policy programs. A good ruler effectively channels the zest of the young people of his country.

On religion: "Man's disquiet is such that he absolutely needs the vagueness and mystery that religion provides him." Napoleon strikes an existential note here. Man doesn't live by bread alone. Without the orienting—if vague—myths of religion, human hearts feel restless.

People who rely too much on logical systems lose wars: "There are men who, because of their physical and moral constitution, tend to schematize everything: whatever their knowledge, intellect, or courage, nature has not brought them here to command an army." War demands that you drop your logical schematics and roll with instinct when necessary.

On reputation: "A great reputation is a great noise; the more you make, the more it spreads: laws, nations, monuments—everything crumbles, but the reputation remains." Napoleon was a man obsessed with leaving his mark on history—in this task, his success cannot be overstated.

On genius: "Misfortune is the midwife of genius." The education system wants to churn out smart and more capable humans—but perhaps no amount of training can pull out a person's best as well as a brush with tragedy.

Napoleon: "You only believe that which it pleases you to believe." Here, Napoleon gives us an early formulation of the *confirmation bias*—only experimentally validated in the 1960s. People interpret new information so that it fits their pre-existing worldviews.

Napoleon lived and fought through the French Revolution. **He wrote: "The nobility would have survived if it had known how to master the writing desk."** Public opinion ended nobility as much as violent force. The nobility failed to convince the public that it served a valuable role.

On Democracy and Despotism: "Democratic governments border on anarchy, monarchy on despotism. Anarchy is powerless; despotism can do great things." Napoleon believed more in the madness of crowds, as supposed to their wisdom: "The people must be saved against their will."

Yet, mere despotic force isn't enough: "You can only lead a people by showing them a future; a leader trades in hope." Napoleon was well aware that "nothing has been founded merely by the sword." He understood that a leader must know how to inspire hope, not just fear.

On Courage: "Courage can't be counterfeited—it's a virtue which escapes hypocrisy." Courage with logical thought is unbeatable: "The burst of courage which, despite the suddenness of events, still leaves you capable of thought, of judgment and decision, is excessively rare."

Napoleon on his destiny: "A superior power pushes me towards a goal of which I know nothing; as long as it has not been attained I am invulnerable, unshakeable; as soon as I am no longer necessary for it, a single step will suffice to topple me."

On Superstitions: "Superstitions are the legacy left by one century's clever people to the fools of the future." Superstitions are mental shortcuts which are helpful when a detailed explanation would be too time-consuming. But superstitions ossify and become counter-productive.

Napoleon on how he planned wars: "There is no man more pusillanimous than I when I am planning a campaign." In the planning stage, Napoleon exaggerated, in his mind "all the dangers and calamities" possible. But while *fighting*, he forgot everything "except what led to success."

Napoleon's relationship with power: "I too love power—but I love it as an artist. I love it as a musician loves his violin. I love it for the sake of drawing sounds, chords, and harmonies from it." Napoleon sought power not for the sake of control, but to create something *new*.

How to police: **"The art of the police consists in punishing rarely and severely.**" Power should mostly be invisible from people's everyday lives: "Authority should make itself felt as little as possible and should not weigh on the people needlessly."

Those who abuse power ultimately taste their own medicine: "A sultan who cut off heads from caprice, would quickly lose his own in the same way. Excesses tend to check themselves by reason of their own violence. What the ocean gains in one place it loses in another."

Napoleon on love: "The ivy clings to the first tree it meets. This, in a few words, is the story of love." The surprise and satisfaction of first love is hard to shake off. To love another person is to fall into their gravity—a lot depends on who we happen to meet *first*.

On Louis XVI, who was executed by guillotine in the French Revolution, Napoleon had this to say: "When Louis XVI was put on trial, he should have simply said that according to law his person was sacred, and left it at that. This would not have saved his life, but he would've died a king."

Napoleon on the permanence of aristocracies: "Among nations and in revolutions, aristocracy always exists. If you attempt to get rid of it by destroying the nobility, it immediately re-establishes itself among the rich and powerful families of the third estate. Destroy it there, and it survives and takes refuge among the leaders of workmen and of the people." **Instead of trying to erase aristocracies, an intelligent ruler gets ideological buy-in from them**: "A prince gains nothing by this shifting of aristocracy. On the contrary he re-establishes stable conditions by permitting it to continue as it is, readjusting, however, the old order to the new principles."

Napoleon on how intelligence has become the main tool in the tool kit of leaders: "Intelligence precedes force. Force itself is nothing without intelligence. In the heroic age the leader was the strongest man, with civilization he has become *the most intelligent of the brave*." Or the bravest of the intelligent?

Contradicting your own decisions is a terrible leak of energy. It also hollows out your authority in front of your inferiors. Napoleon: "The thing to avoid is not so much error as self-contradiction. It is especially by the latter that authority loses its force." Only the decisive will win high stakes games.

Idleness and doubting yourself are two great dangers: "We are made weak both by idleness and distrust of ourselves. Unfortunate, indeed, is he who suffers from both. If he is a mere individual he becomes nothing; if he is a king he is lost." People aim to increase their wealth, their muscle mass, their social media followers...and all three have great utility. But here's another metric to maximize: your self-belief. Drag your idleness and self-doubt as close to zero as you can, and you'll do great things.

Do not assume you need reason to sway men; it is often absurdities that hold the strongest sway over large groups of people: "One is more certain to influence men, to produce more effect on them, by absurdities than by sensible ideas." Absurd ideas, shot through with poetry, exaggeration, and humor, will catch on better than the truth, presented logically.

Bold moves win the day when prudence cannot: "Prudence is good when one has the choice of means. When one hasn't, it is daring which achieves success."

Napoleon: "Display is to power what ceremony is to religion." Just like abstract religious principles need to be codified and embodied via ceremonies...power needs to be codified and embodied via occasional flashy displays.

Stop being impressionable. Only listening to your own judgment is the mark of a superior mind: "The superior man is not by nature impressionable. We praise him, we blame him; it matters little to him. It is to his own judgment that he listens." (A revealing anecdote: Napoleon was greeted like a rockstar when passing through Switzerland in 1798. It must be nice to be so passionately admired, his colleague said. Napoleon: "Bah! This same unthinking crowd, under a slight change of circumstances, would follow me just as eagerly to the scaffold."

PART THREE

C FOR
CIVILIZATION

28

HOW DEMOCRACY REPRESSES
EXCELLENCE

A Mencken Chrestomathy, 1949

H.L. Mencken was among the very first English translators of Nietzsche. His productivity was legendary: he wrote more than 10 million words over his lifetime. He hated the modern age, opposed the New Deal, and was against American entry into WW-II. Mencken's most powerful idea: Democracy is not a solution but a *problem.* Dig in:

Early democrats didn't care for "the democratic ideal" at all. They had "highly materialistic" demands instead: "more to eat, less work, higher wages, lower taxes." The masses didn't wish to "exterminate the baron" but only to make him fulfill his "baronial" duties.

Deep down, humans crave hierarchy. The French Revolution exemplified this craving. Mencken: "The Paris proletariat, having been misled into killing its King in 1793, devoted the next two years to killing those who had misled it—by the middle of 1796 it had another

King...with an attendant herd of barons, counts, marquises, dukes."

Democracy *intensifies* groupthink and group identity: "Democratic man is quite unable to think of himself as a free individual; he must belong to a group, or shake with fear and loneliness—and the group, of course, must have its leaders." More groups = more leaders.

Freud said we repress our sex drive as it's frowned upon, but there's nothing that democracy frowns upon more than clear proof of superiority. Democracy says "the most worthy and laudable citizen is that one who is most like all the rest." Hence we repress our urge to excel.

Democracies have the aristocracy of money—Mencken calls them "plutocrats." But the plutocracy "lacks all the essential characteristics of a true aristocracy: a clean tradition, culture, public spirit, honesty, honor, courage—above all, courage. It is transient and lacks a goal." The plutocrats lack "an aristocratic disinterestedness born of aristocratic security."

Democracies birth their intellectual apologists—Mencken calls them "pedagogues." These are not genuine thinkers; they're "men chiefly marked by their haunting fear of losing their jobs." The pedagogue's job is to ensure adherence to the latest law dreamt up by the mob or the plutocrats. Mencken: "The pedagogue, in the long run, shows the virtues of the Congressman, the newspaper editorial writer or the butler, not those of the aristocrat."

Our age demands we repress our greatness. Mencken: "A man who has throttled a bad impulse has at least some consolation in his agonies. But a man who has throttled a good one is in a bad way indeed. Yet this great Republic swarms with such men, and their sufferings are under every eye."

Democracy lives on envy. Mencken: "No doubt my distaste for democracy as a political theory is, like every other human prejudice, due to an inner lack—to a defect that is a good deal less in the theory than in myself. In this case it is very probably my incapacity for envy."

Mencken on the two worst crimes in a democracy: "There is only one sound argument for democracy, and that is the argument that it is a crime for any man to hold himself out as better than other men, and, above all, a most heinous offense for him to prove it."

Mencken explains the difference between Feudalism and Democracy: "The essential objection to feudalism was that it imposed degrading acts and attitudes upon the vassal; the essential objection to democracy is that it imposes degrading acts and attitudes upon the men responsible for the welfare and dignity of the state."

To gain power in a democracy, men sacrifice their self-respect. Mencken: "The democratic politician, confronted by the dishonesty and stupidity of his master, the mob, tries to convince himself and all the rest of us that it is really full of rectitude and wisdom."

Democracy is not friendly to truth as the mob prefers pliable lies to immovable facts. H.L. Mencken: "Truth has a harshness that alarms them, and an air of finality that collides with their incurable romanticism."

If democrats are so sure they have the right answer, why do they abandon their "whole philosophy" and become "despots" at the "first sign of strain"? Mencken: "I need not point to what happens invariably in democratic states when the national safety is menaced." When a true calamity, such as war, strikes, voting is inevitably suspended. Curious.

Mencken believed that over the long-term, democracy might cancel itself out: "For all I know, democracy may be a self-limiting disease, as civilization itself seems to be. There are thumping paradoxes in its philosophy, and some of them have a suicidal smack."

29

FEMINISM'S 5 MAJOR MISTAKES

What's Wrong With the World? 1910

Feminism is not a law of nature. It's not a scientific fact. It's a *political* ideology. The pro-feminist arguments are just that: arguments. They can be challenged, attacked, and refuted. That's what G.K. Chesterton did more than a hundred years ago in his 1910 book: **What's Wrong With the World?** We will explore his arguments here.

Here's how you know an ideology has truly won: You feel a vague sense of fear spread in your body at the mere prospect of criticizing it. That's how the average person feels when entertaining mildly anti-feminist thoughts. The fear is not unfounded, for to attack feminism is to attack the central political dogma of our time. But this dogma won without being strong. It walks around on tottering feet, and G.K. Chesterton attacked its kneecaps with hammers. Let's see how:

Feminism's first mistake: In traditional societies, women weren't *denied* work. They were *spared* work. The feminist conception of working is absurdly romantic. The reality is that work drains your time, energy, and your very spirit. Chesterton writes that the traditional arrangement of keeping women out of offices and factories protected them from "harassing industrial demands." Women were shielded from the "direct cruelty of competitive or bureaucratic toil." Until very recently in human history, work meant pollution, odors, physical pain, headaches, and an increased risk of death. For hundreds of millions of men around the world in 2024, that is *still* what work means. Women were not wholesale denied something great. They were wholesale protected from something terrible.

Feminism's second mistake: Housework isn't narrower than "real work," it's broader. The feminists have it backward. They argue that real work outside home is creative and empowering while housework is repetitive drudgery. But the economy actually rewards you for mastering one thing and repeating it till you drop dead. The website designer must design a thousand websites. The logo designer must dream of circles and dots. The Japanese cook must make sushi till the sun explodes. The singer must sing his *one* hit song till his throat bursts. But a mother can go from designing her son's scarf to baking him a cookie to singing him a lullaby *all* in the same evening. She's a designer, a cook, a singer, and a hundred other professions. Now whose work is broader? Chesterton: "The world outside the home was one mass of narrowness, a maze of cramped paths, a madhouse of monomaniacs." It is no punishment to be denied entry to a madhouse.

Feminism's third mistake: Women were correctly kept out of politics because abstract thinking is difficult, if not impossible, for them.

Why does the law wear blindfolds? To think in abstractions. To ignore personal details that matter not. To focus on facts instead of feelings. To reduce reality to the provable and dispense justice accordingly. Civilization requires custodians who can be fair, harsh, and blind when necessary. But women lack this skill set.

Individuals have a thousand idiosyncrasies, sure. Each a truly unique soul. The female mind is sensitive to this fact. She cannot help but pay attention to the individual quirks, the personal context...the *particular* backstories that drive *particular* humans. But you cannot rule a country without common laws, common standards, and impartial judgment. Men and women may have unique idiosyncratic souls, but they cannot have unique idiosyncratic constitutions.

Chesterton wrote that women have a "hesitation about absolute rules." This hesitation is good, even "wholesome," in some domains. You can't have absolute rules when you have 5 kids with wildly different personalities, needs, and abilities. But you need absolute rules at the scale of nations. You need to stand by your laws and your principles—and punish those who attack them—if civilization is to be stable.

Feminism's fourth mistake: Offices are less free than homes, not more. Chesterton: "The woman's work is to some small degree creative and individual. She can put the furniture in fancy arrangements of her own. I fear the bricklayer cannot put the bricks in fancy arrangements of his own, without disaster to himself and others. A woman cooking may not always cook artistically; still she *can* cook artistically. She can introduce a personal and imperceptible alteration into the composition of a soup. The clerk is not encouraged to introduce a personal and imperceptible alteration into the figures in a ledger." The traditional home was not a prison but a walled garden. Outside the walls was compulsion, grind, and mechanical drudgery. Inside the walls was love, life, and the freedom to tinker.

Feminism's fifth mistake: Civilization cannot do without generalist people and generalist tools.

Chesterton uses the example of tools like fire and sticks to show why generalists matter.

A stick is a worse weapon than a gun, but a better walking pole. It's a worse measuring tool than a marked tape, but a better weapon. It's not the best tool for anything, but it's wonderfully versatile for everyday life. Fire has the same versatility: it cooks your food, warms you, lights your path, and scares the animal trying to kill you. Just like generalist tools are important for life, so are generalist people.

Chesterton: "Tradition has decided that only half of humanity shall be monomaniac. It has decided that in every home there shall be a tradesman and a

Jack-of-all-trades. But it has also decided that the Jack-of-all-trades shall be a Jill-of-all-trades."

Women had handled the generalist mantle since the beginning of history until feminism started making absurd demands on them. Chesterton writes: "I do not deny that women have been wronged and even tortured; but I doubt if they were ever tortured so much as they are tortured now by the absurd modern attempt to make them domestic empresses and competitive clerks at the same time."

Go read the entire book: *What's Wrong With The World.* It's wonderfully funny and every sentence glistens with insight.

30

TWISTING MINDS, 101

Propaganda, 1965

Jacques Ellul was a French theologian. He was an incisive critic of technology, media, and the interface between the two. His 1965 book on propaganda has only gotten truer. Here are its 11 most important ideas:

Breaking news is breaking minds. When everything is urgent, you are forced to "remain on the surface of the event." Ellul on how the modern man lacks a center of gravity: "Lacking landmarks, he follows all currents." His soul is "discontinuous and fragmented." Life is reduced to unconnected moments...

Jacques Ellul predicted echo chambers: "Those who read the press of their group and listen to the radio of their group are constantly reinforced in their allegiance." Even the stupidest idea will start feeling believable if everyone around you reinforces it all day, everyday.

Modern man can "never stop to reflect." He's not allowed to synthesize his information. Rather, Ellul writes: "One thought drives away another; old facts are chased by new ones."

Clear thought has been replaced by vague feeling: "Modern man does not think about current problems; he feels them. He reacts, but he does not understand them any more than he takes responsibility for them."

Everyone can read but not everyone can think. This makes propaganda more, not less, common. Ellul: "The vast majority of people, perhaps 90 percent, know how to read, but do not exercise their intelligence beyond this. They attribute authority and eminent value to the printed word...they are precisely on the level at which the printed word can seize and convince them without opposition."

Once a person is compromised...once they've acted out a lie...they are yours forever. Ellul: "He who acts in obedience to propaganda can never go back. He is now obliged to believe in that propaganda because of his past action. He is obliged to receive from it his justification and authority, without which his action will seem to him absurd or unjust, which would be intolerable."

Propagandists work by channeling the energies of "fundamentals myths." They hijack the collective mind by playing on shared narratives such as "the myth of happiness, the myth of progress, the myth of the nation." A skilled propagandist will always borrow from, and build on, the "current beliefs and symbols" of a society.

Propagandists set up "psychological levers." They ensure that "certain words, signs or symbols" start provoking certain reflex actions...and then they wait. The levers can now be turned when and how needed.

Indirect propaganda works best. Aggressive attempts at manipulation will fail as people's defenses will go up. But give a man plausible deniability, feed him convenient information, make him feel that he's "obeying reason" as he follows your command, and you have him where you want him.

Lonely, depressed people are the easiest victims of propaganda. Jacques Ellul: "An individual can be influenced by forces such as propaganda only when he is cut off from membership in local groups because such groups are organic and have a well-structured material, spiritual and emotional life; they are not easily penetrated by propaganda."

The conditions of modern life are very propaganda-friendly: "The permanent uncertainty, the social mobility, the absence of sociological protection and of traditional frames of reference — all these inevitably provide propaganda with a malleable environment that can be conditioned at will. The individual left to himself is defenseless..."

31

HOW "MANAGERS" RULE THE WORLD

The Managerial Revolution, 1941

70 years ago, James Burnham predicted the world we live in. He saw that capitalism would die, and socialism *won't* replace it. Instead, a new elite will take over—The Managers. Top ten insights from his prophetic book:

Capitalism ruled for the past few centuries and was supported by concepts such as "individualism, private initiative, natural rights" and so on. But Burnham sees that capitalism has lost the "boundless self-confidence" that an ideology needs to rule.

The world today is increasingly led by managers. This is evident in the push for a new "pattern of thought and feeling" that benefits the managerial class: the emphasis on individuals shifts to "the people," and private initiative gives way to "planning."

Who are the managers? The managers are the "administrators, experts, directing engineers, production executives, propaganda specialists, and technocrats." These managers sideline the capitalist owners under the pretext of their greed, and the masses under the pretext of their ignorance.

The center of power has moved from parliaments to bureaus. Elected representatives wielded real power in the past. Today, real power lies with the unelected managers in "bureaus, executive agencies, and commissions." Even wars are waged by a "Pentagon-style managerial bureaucracy." Burnham: "Parliament was the sovereign body of the LIMITED state of capitalism. The bureaus are the sovereign bodies of the UNLIMITED state of managerial society." Today, life is enmeshed with the "rules, regulations, laws, decrees" emerging from different bureaus.

Where are the managers? Everywhere. In the US, "non-teaching" administrators have grown by 138% since 1978—students enrolled have grown by 8%. The number of doctors has grown by 150% since 1975—number of "hospital administrators" by 3,200%. The people who do actual work are a shrinking minority in corporations. They are outvoiced, outvoted, and overpowered by the managerial class.

Managerialism always gets out of hand. In 1941 Burnham wrote that the manager class is "inbred and self justifying." Operations are kept alive "which have little social purpose other than to nourish an enclave of managers."

Managerialism is also anti-democratic. Burnham writes that capitalism is democratic as "no one group" controls the whole economy." Opposing factions such as agriculture, industry, labor, capital, etc fight it out. But in the managerial state, a "single integrated set of institutions" controls all.

How can we fight managerialism? Burnham saw no optimistic future and the power of the managers has only ballooned since he wrote the book. But the solution might lie in playing the managers off each other so they can't "spend all their time managing the rest of us." Whatever it takes, Burnham wrote, people should try to save their "national individuality" from getting "dissolved into the global managerial state."

32

WHY SOCIETIES NEED MYTHS

Textos I, 1959

Nicolás Gómez Dávila had a chance to be chief advisor to the Colombian President. He rejected the offer and built a library with 30,000 books instead. His own obscure book—only 100 copies were printed—has brilliant insights into how societies are held up by myths and fall without them. Dig in:

A culture that ignores its distinct DNA, and embraces homogenization, is signing its own death warrant. Dávila: "Violence is not necessary to destroy a civilization. Each civilization dies from indifference toward the unique values which created it."

The opposite of myth is not rationality, but shallowness: "The enemies of myth are not the friends of reality but of triviality." Myths deal with deep and timeless questions—to throw all myths out of the window is to only be left with trivial queries.

On the condition of modernity: "The modern tragedy is not the tragedy of reason defeated but of reason triumphant." Reason is a useful tool, but it can't become the sole yardstick for judging every aspect of life. We don't suffer from irrationality but over-rationality.

Are your emotions genuine? Or are they hiding spots where you seek refuge from something unbearable? Dávila: "Modern man does not love, but seeks refuge in love; does not hope, but seeks refuge in hope; does not believe, but seeks refuge in a dogma."

Are you actually free or do you just never venture far enough to feel the noose around the neck? Dávila: "Modern man is a prisoner who thinks he is free because he refrains from touching the walls of his dungeon." Stay inside the overton window and you can pick the iPhone color.

Dávila: "In an age in which the media broadcast countless pieces of foolishness, the educated man is defined not by what he knows, but by what he doesn't know." Being uninformed is better than being ill-informed by an incompetent and corrupt press.

Dávila on contemporary architecture: "In the idiom of modern architecture nothing complicated can be said." The apparently superfluous details of classical architecture are actually ways to *capture* complex ideas. The brute minimalism of contemporary architecture leaves no room for subtext.

Dávila: "Modern man destroys more when he builds than when he destroys." Destruction just leaves emptiness behind, but *built* ugliness actively pollutes the world.

Dávila on the cyclical nature of political history: "Ideas of the left give birth to revolutions. Revolutions give birth to ideas of the right." Idealism without realism creates disastrous revolutions that only hard-nosed pragmatists can salvage anything from.

This aphorism from Dávila made my head spin for 2 days: "The genuine coherence of our ideas does not come from the reasoning that ties them together, but from the spiritual impulse that gives rise to them." Your unified worldview won't come from logic but a deeper impulse.

Dávila's important warning: "Those who proclaim that the noble is despicable end up by proclaiming that the despicable is noble." A society that cannot defend its noble from its despicable has no future.

A great sense of loss permeates all of Dávila's aphorisms: "Civilization seems to be the invention of a species now extinct."

Sharing the same worldview is an essential precondition to productive dialogue: "To have a dialogue with those who do not share our basic premises is nothing more than a stupid way to kill time." What do shared basic premises look like at the scale of a nation? Like myths.

Beauty is a rare, fragile, and temporary spark lit against the unending darkness of the ugly, the uninspiring, the mid. Dávila: "All ages exhibit the same vices, but not all show the same virtues. In every age there are hovels, but only in some are there palaces."

33

10 CONCEPTS THAT EXPLAIN THE MODERN WORLD

Parkinson's Law: Companies become bigger and worse over time. Tasks expand to fill up the allotted time. Clerks manufacture work for each other as overall capacity dips. When British Navy ships went down from 68 to 20, officials increased by 78%.

Chesterton Fence: If you don't know what an old custom does, don't touch it. It may be holding back problems you're completely unaware of. You've not seen the wolves yet because of the very fence you're about to demolish.

The Medici Effect: Sculptors, painters, and architects converged in Florence as the Medicis were funding the artists. Their proximity led to a fertile dialogue which, in turn, led to the Renaissance. Will the internet lead to a new cultural era by amplifying the cross-pollination of ideas?

The Centipede's Dilemma: Ask a centipede which one of its hundred legs moves the fastest and it forgets how to move. Reflecting on what we normally do without thought ironically worsens performance. A culture of endless self-reflection, therapy, and navel gazing is eroding important life skills.

Tyranny of small decisions: Individuals make small decisions to maximize convenience but this leads to massive social failure. We nod along to contagious ideas like "gender is fluid" because resisting them is too much work—till kids start getting transgender surgery. The slippery slope is not a fallacy but a fundamental reality.

The Zebra Effect explains why people don't want to stand out. Zebras are hard to individually study as it's nearly impossible to track one of them for long (lost in the striped chaos). So scientists once put a big red dot on one zebra so he could be tracked and studied. Lions zeroed in on him and hunted him with ease. Getting lost among others is a survival mechanism. Hence the human desire to conform.

Why the ruler can't rule: The executive head can't implement his ideas on ground because the bureaucrats are closer to it, and have an agenda of their own. The Tzar of Russia had to deal with the Deep State too. Nicholas II: "I never ruled Russia. 10,000 clerks ruled Russia."

Gall's law: A complex system that works is invariably found to have evolved from a simple system that worked. Only fools and modern technocrats try to create complex systems from scratch.

Minimal Self Hypothesis: Narcissism is a "strategic retreat" into the safety of one's own self. When the future looks random, inexplicable, and informationally overwhelming, people enter survival mode. The self becomes "minimal" to reduce its surface area to pain. People today are giving up on commitment of all sorts to conserve energy for vague and upcoming disasters.

Tetris Syndrome: The world will eventually start looking like Tetris blocks if you play the game too much. What we do most often becomes the metaphor through which we look at the world. Takeaway: Most people today are addicted to their 2D phones—and this will hurt the general aptitude for dealing with the 3D world.

9 REASONS WHY ARISTOCRACY BEATS DEMOCRACY

The Pleasures of Philosophy, 1929

Will Durant is perhaps the best-selling historian of all time. He spent his life learning, teaching, and writing history. He still has readers in high places—Elon Musk recommends his 11 volume set, *The Story of Civilization*. In this chapter, I've curated Will Durant's insights on aristocracy. Most modern people have only ever known life under democracy, so it's useful to do a comparative analysis. The quotes come from Will's 1929 book, *The Pleasures of Philosophy*.

The Freedom Paradox. Will Durant writes that while aristocracies do limit "political freedom," democracies are no freer as they crush individuality with the "fanatic pressure of dull majorities." Better a rule by minorities trained from the "outset" in the rigors of an aristocratic upbringing.

The Pyramid Problem. Will Durant said there are grand tasks "requiring generations" of coordination and democracy is utterly incapable of them. A democratically elected leader can never build a Pyramid.

Pedigree versus Pocketbooks: Will Durant writes that "rule by pedigree is the only alternative to rule by pocketbooks." Rich oligarchs always subject nations to the "ideals of the stock exchange, the marketplace, and the factory" unless aristocrats stop them.

Elections are Lotteries: Aristocracies free leaders from the "lottery of elections." French philosopher Renan predicted that elections will be the triumph of "mediocrity" as they'll put "knaves and quacks upon the throne."

The Case of England: "England's leaders were trained for public place from their boyhood; first at home, then at Eton or Harrow, then at Oxford or Cambridge, and then by appointment to arduous minor offices. It was these men who lifted little England to the top of the world."

Slow is fast: Will Durant writes that societies cannot change too quickly because "large bodies must move slowly." But what about science progressing rapidly? The analogy breaks down when you understand that "society is not a laboratory, and men do not submit to vivisection." Science thrives on trial and error; doing trial and error in political affairs racks up the body count in millions. Ask Chairman Mao.

Traditions as Memory. Will Durant writes: "The sanity of the individual lies in the continuity of his memory; the sanity of a group lies in the continuity of its traditions." Progressives are strangely proud of their amnesia.

Aristocracy of the soul. Will Durant defines the "aristocracy of soul": "A vigor and yet ease of carriage, a sureness of touch in judgment and taste, a readiness of wit, an unassuming dignity and an unfailing generosity."

The Aristocratic Peace. Will Durant writes that equality is the breeding ground of violence: "Peace is between unequals; the pretense of equality brings a perennial tug of war." Only by accepting the "natural inequality of men in intellect and will" can we realize the "hypocrisy of egalitarian institutions." Aristocratic peace demands that we do not lie.

35

10 LAWS OF BIG SYSTEMS

Systemantics: How Systems Work and Especially How They Fail, 1975

John Gall explains corporate dysfunction, government waste, and civilizational collapse with one sweeping theory in Systematics. *Systems*, he writes, throw *antics*—hence the title. Gall approaches his daunting topic with a sense of humor. He distills his complicated ideas into pithy, memorable one-liners. Systematics came out in 1976 and has since acquired a cult following. Jordan Peterson recommends it.

Here are 10 laws of big systems. They will help you understand the world around you a lot better:

Law 1: "New systems mean new problems." A government agency that moves from paper to digital records is suddenly vulnerable to cyber-attacks and data theft. What they gained in speed, they may have lost in security. This is not to say that the world should be analog—but that every new solution births new problems, which then have to be tackled. Proposed new systems, new regulations, and new products should be analyzed via the Downstream Consequences Razor: If this new thing is loosed on the world, what will be the downstream consequences? What are some possible negative spill offs?

Law 2: "Systems Don't Go Away, and since they occupy space, our landscape is now littered with the bleached bones and rotting carcasses of old attempted solutions to our problems." In South Carolina you need a license to braid hair. In India there's a law against the unlawful possession of "telegraph wires" which stopped existing decades ago. In many countries around the world, you can run into trouble with authorities for setting down a fence on your *own* land due to zoning laws. Systems don't automatically go away, no matter how outdated they get. They need to be manually struck down—a process that is always cumbersome, and therefore never attractive. Everyday, people lose their valuable energy and time just to navigate around *regulatory litter.*

Law 3: "A trance-like state, a suspension of normal mental activity, induced by membership within a System." Once inside a system, you have a vested interest to keep it going. Not only is it paying your bills, it's also giving you structure, meaning, and identity. A place in the world. A mission to go on. And therefore you go into a "trance-like state"—you stop engaging with reality. You see the world via the lens of The System. This means thousands of people can develop the same blindspot once they're in the same system. Disconnecting with reality is a small price to pay for the warm glow of tribal affiliation.

Law 4: "Systems are seductive." Here's John Gall's brilliant explanation: "They promise to do a hard job faster, better, and more easily than you could do it by yourself. But if you set up a System, you are likely to find your time and effort now being consumed in the care and feeding of the System itself. New Problems are created by its very presence. Once set up, it won't Go Away; it Grows and Encroaches. It begins to do Strange and Wonderful Things and Breaks Down in Ways You Never Thought Possible. It Kicks Back, Gets In The Way and Opposes Its Own Proper Function. Your own perspective becomes distorted by being In The System. You become anxious and Push On It To Make It Work. Eventually you come to believe that the misbegotten product it so grudgingly delivers is What You Really Wanted all the time. At that point, Encroachment has become complete. You have become absorbed. You are now a Systems-person."

Law 5: "Systems don't work for you or for me. They work for their own goals." The official task of a government education department is to improve educational outcomes, but its unofficial mission is to make education slower, less efficient, and more wasteful to feed its own bureaucratic expansion. In name, the military exists to protect against external foes—in practice the military mostly exists to prop up the military-industrial complex. As John Gall notes: "The system itself does not do what it says it is doing. The name is most emphatically not the thing." Systems behave like they have a "will to live" *independent* of the intentions with which they were initially set up.

Law 6: "You're always inside a system. The only question is: Which?"

John Gall explains how bad systems, and the people inside them, slowly go insane: "A poorly-functioning System begins to generate increasing numbers of messages, often shaped around such questions as "What went wrong?", "How far along is Task X?", and especially, "Why don't we have better feedback?" As the System sinks deeper and deeper into the morass of unfinished tasks, the business of exchanging messages expands exponentially, until at last the non-functioning System is completely occupied with its own internal communication processes. Like a catatonic schizophrenic, it is now preoccupied with a fantasy life that is completely internal."

Law 7: "Avoid unnecessary systems. Do it with an existing system if you can. Do it with a small system if you can." John Gall advises minimalism. The smaller and fewer the systems, the lesser the chance of unexpected interactions, strange cross-overs, and runaway complications.

Law 8: "The message sent is not necessarily the message received." Communication breaks down. Information "decays" inside systems. The boss's orders are misunderstood by his managers. Their orders are then misheard by the employees, who then misunderstand each other. This game of Chinese whispers happens at all levels, all the time.

Law 9: "Loose systems last longer and function better." Take two hypothetical companies: company A and company B. Company A has 50 generalists and 50 specialists, while Company B has 90 specialists and only 10 generalists. Company A is a comparatively loose system while company B is tighter and more focussed. In a favorable economic niche, company B will outcompete company A. But if economic winds suddenly shift, and the market demands a big change in direction, then company B will get outclassed. Its specialists—good at just one thing—will struggle to adapt. The generalists of Company A, on the other hand, will be able to reposition and reinvent themselves for the new world. Loose systems win in the long-term.

Law 10: "Avoid uphill configurations. Systems run best when designed to run downhill." Communism failed for many reasons—one of them was that it expected people to behave like selfless saints. But people won't stop being people just because your system demands it. Uphill systems are tiresome because they go against human nature. John Gall explains how national lotteries keep generating steady revenue even in economic downturns because people are always willing to bet something small in order to win something big—no matter how slim the odds. It's a system downhill from human psychology, and so it works.

Three final takeaways from Systemantics:

- "Systems attract systems-people."

- "A complex system that works is invariably found to have evolved from a simple system that worked."

- "In setting up a new system, tread softly. You may be disturbing another system that is actually working."

36

THE TWO-PUNCH COMBO THAT TOOK OUT ROME: PANEM ET CIRCENSES

The City In History, 1961

Ancient Rome was the world's most powerful empire for 500 years. At its height, Rome boasted of roads, public baths, and much else that was close to miraculous for the rest of the planet. Then came the Great Fall. What happened has lessons for the world today. Dig in:

In his book *The City In History*, Lewis Mumford explains how Rome went from "Megalopolis to Necropolis." This great city set up its own demise in two ways: Panem et circenses. That is: "bread and circuses." Mumford: "Success underwrote a sickening parasitic failure."

As Rome became prosperous, it became an unsustainable welfare state. Mumford writes that "indiscriminate public largesse" became common. A large portion of the population "took on the parasitic role for a whole lifetime."

More than 200,000 citizens of Rome regularly received handouts of bread from "public storehouses." The desire to lead an industrious productive life had severely "weakened." So what did people spend their time on? Distractions, which meant circuses.

The Roman people, not working for their livelihood but living off of the prosperity of their city, became *numb*. Mumford: "To recover the bare sensation of being alive, the Roman populace, high and low, governors and governed, flocked to the great arenas" for games and distractions.

The entertainment included "chariot races, spectacular naval battles set in an artificial lake, theatrical pantomimes in which lewder sexual acts were performed." Out of 365 days, more than 200 were public holidays and 93 were "devoted to games at the public expense."

Consuming entertainment became the primary priority of Roman citizens in Rome's decadent phase: "Not to be present at the show was to be deprived of life, liberty, and happiness." Concrete concerns of life became "subordinate, accessory, almost meaningless."

Rome could put half of its total population "in its circuses and theaters" at the same time! A new public holiday was declared to celebrate every military victory. But the number of holidays kept rising even when Rome's military prowess began to fail...

Mumford writes that no empire had such an "abundance of idle time to fill with idiotic occupations." Even the

Roman emperors who privately despised the games had to pretend they enjoyed them for "fear of hostile public response."

Bottom line. The very power and prosperity of Ancient Rome set the stage for its collapse. As welfare states expand around the world today, and entertainment options get ever more immersive, we are forced to ask a question: Is our Post-Industrial Civilization...Rome, Part II?

37

THE TERRIBLE GULF BETWEEN
MALE AND FEMALE NATURE

Sexual Personae, 1991

It's futile to talk of *human* nature without exploring the difference between *male* and *female* nature. "Humankind" is a childish liberal fantasy. There is mankind, there is womankind, and there's nothing else.

The best thinker on this topic is Camille Paglia. Her grand theory of the gulf between male and female nature is as provocative as it is rigorously argued. She lays it out in great length in her magnum opus, *Sexual Personae* (1991). Here are the book's top insights.

Paglia: "Sexual physiology (sets) the pattern for our experience of the world." The man's penis underlines "linearity, focus, aim, directedness." Men are goal-oriented animals, and goals make the world *binary*. Success and failure. If you want food, you either get fed or you starve. If you want to win an Olympic medal, you're either on the podium or you're not. The male world is either-or. The female world is not.

This is because nature, Paglia argues, forces females to make peace with *hidden* genitals—which makes them comfortable with "greater subjectivity." Paglia's argument is that your sexual organs determine your *existential* disposition. Note how the *ultimate* female book, written by a woman *for* other women *only,* is called 50 Shades of *Gray.* Coincidence?

Note how as more women entered academia in the past century, it became *subjective*—that is, *feminine.* Relativism came rushing in. Postmodernism became the dominant academic lens. The binary of right and wrong was thrown out as regressive. The question of whether two and two *really* add up to four was mocked by George Orwell in *1984* as the absolute limit of dystopian *absurdity.* In 2024, the same question is earnestly asked by Harvard mathematicians like Kareem Carr. He says it might as well be five. He's a man, but to discredit basic logic, reject the binary of right and wrong, and inject ambiguity where it does not belong is a profoundly feminine instinct.

Men and women view the world differently, act differently in it, and these differences are rooted in their distinct sexual biology. No amount of social engineering can cancel out these differences. **Even our views of history are different**: Paglia writes that since females are intimate with their monthly cycles, their view of history is cyclical. Male history is "evolutionary history"—a "propulsive movement into the future."

Paglia on women: "Physically and psychologically, they are serenely self-contained. They may choose to achieve, but they do not need it." Men, however, must "quest, pursue, court, or seize." (She writes art is the "closest man has come to imitating" a woman's procreative powers. More on this later.)

Civilization is Male; Nature is Female

Civilization is a male project to tame and channel the chaotic energies of nature.

Paglia calls civilization *Apollonian*, and the chaos of nature *Dionysian*. Apollo was the Greek God of order, logic, and light. Dionysus was the God of chaos, wine, fertility, and insanity. For Paglia, men are apollonian while women are dionysian.

Nature and females both are knots of creation and destruction, uncontrollable and unknowable, more *energy* than *order*. **In a natural disaster people instinctively refer to the "wrath of Mother Earth."** Nature is neither benevolent nor hostile but psychotically amoral.

The Apollonian male spirit tries to order nature's chaos. You can think of civilization as a male attempt to *escape* Mother nature. Paglia: "If civilization had been left in female hands, we'd still be living in grass huts." Instead we have towering castles, skyscrapers, roads running for thousands of miles, and satellites in outer space. Such a civilization is not possible without the *linear* thinking, *binary* mindset and the *propulsive* restlessness of the male mind. (Of course it's not possible without new life either, which women have an outsized role in creating and nurturing.)

Paglia on the battle between civilization and nature: "Society is an artificial construction, a defense against nature's power. Without society, we would be storm-tossed on the barbarous sea that is nature. Society is a system of inherited forms reducing our humiliating passivity to nature."

For Paglia, the male-female dynamic mirrors the civilization-nature dynamic. In both cases, there's a "push and pull of attraction and hostility." The female has a monopoly on creating life but it *needs* the apollonian civilization, built by men, if life is to not get *swamped* by indifferent nature that loves to "throw its weight around."

The male fears the feminine Dionysian spirit for it may wreck his systematic world, the female fears an overbearing Apollonian spirit that may smother her freedom. The male tragedy is suffocating order, the female tragedy is shapeless chaos. An imbalanced Apollo needs an infusion of Dionysian freedom, and an imbalanced Dionysius needs the structure that Apollo provides.

From *Sexual Personae*: "Political equality for women, desirable and necessary as it is, is not going to remedy the radical disjunction between the sexes that begins and ends in the body. The sexes will always be jolted by violent shocks of attraction and repulsion."

Paglia argues that contemporary civilization is becoming dysfunctional because it's over-feminized. Take the "unresolved contradictions" of modern liberalism. On one hand, liberalism denounces all "social orders as oppressive." However, it also "expects the government to provide materially for all, a feat manageable only by an expansion of authority." *Daddy* government must protect the *effeminate* citizen from the terrible *trauma* of mean tweets, but he must be an all-permissive mother otherwise. Paglia: "Liberalism defines government as tyrant father but demands it behave as nurturant mother."

Why Art is Masculine

Paglia has a unique perspective on beauty: "Beauty is our weapon against nature; by it we make objects, giving them limit, symmetry, proportion. Beauty halts and freezes the melting flux of nature." Beauty is one of humanity's great tools—it makes the world more predictable, palatable, and *humane*.

Dionysian nature has no morals, no goal to aim at, and no concern for human desires or suffering. Art is how we try to get a handle on it. Paglia: "The most effective weapon against the flux of nature is art." **Art has order,**

narrative, human agency—everything that nature mocks in her vast indifference. Paglia: "Art is never simply design. It is always a ritualistic reordering of reality." Art, religion, and civilization impose "a graph of marked-off spaces on nature's continuity and flow." Paglia: "We have made Apollonian demarcations that function as ritual preserves against nature." Art draws boundaries on nature to make it more predictable and *homely.*

For Paglia, art, religion, and civilization are man's half-solutions to the eternally chaotic nature: "Religion, ritual, and art began as one." Man chants a hymn, sketches a painting, and erects a city wall for the same reason: to buffer against, and impose his vision, on nature.

Art is about creating order out of chaos, and not promoting a particular morality: "It is the order in morality rather than the morality in order that attracts the artist." An artist's greatest motivation is to make nature's madness coherent using the alchemy of his work.

Art rises from the "deranged egotism and orderliness" of the male mind. Most criminals and geniuses are men because both crime and art involve imposing one's personal masculine will on the world: "There is no female Mozart because there is no female Jack the ripper."

Paglia writes that art is our primal and premiere sense-making tool. Paglia: "Art reflects on and resolves the eternal human dilemma of order versus energy." Nature is "energy, ecstasy, hysteria"—art is the judgmental eye that crafts a coherent story out of it.

38

WHY POLITICS MUST BE THEOLOGICAL

The Nobel Prize Address, 1970

The Harvard Commencement Speech, 1978

The Templeton Prize Address, 1983

Solzhenitsyn lived a great 20th century life. He fought for Stalin in World War II; was sent to the gulag for 8 years because he criticized Stalin in a private letter; married, divorced, re-married, and re-divorced the same woman; KGB poisoned him but he didn't die; won the Nobel Prize for Literature; kicked out of U.S.S.R in 1974; outlived U.S.S.R and went back to Russia in 1994; died a hero to his people and the world. In his 20 year exile from the U.S.S.R, he lived in the west and delivered many lectures. Here are 10 great insights curated from 3 different lectures:

Solzhenitsyn said that the "concepts of good and evil have been ridiculed for several centuries," but no healthy political system can do without them. Without a philosophical good and evil, there's no legal right or wrong. All stable societies are based on a foundational ethic.

Solzhenitsyn calls the contemporary obsession with free trade a "perfect anesthetic." He accuses our age of busying itself with economics to avoid moral questions. Solzhenitsyn says that it has now become "embarrassing to appeal to eternal concepts." All people care for are transient economic considerations. But just as we need a fixed ground to physically move forward, we need a fixed *moral* ground for *moral* progress.

We think of politics in secular terms, but Solzhenitsyn makes a compelling case for bringing the religious angle back into the discussion. If politics feels rootless and circular, he argues it is because we have hacked off its natural religious grounding.

Modern life has two important ailments: "Hastiness and superficiality are the psychic diseases of the twentieth century." People prefer to think and do a lot superficially instead of thinking or doing one thing in depth.

Solzhenitsyn argued that a "decline in courage " was evident in all facets of modern life. From art to politics, from business to education, he noted a certain "depression, passivity, and perplexity" of the spirit. A postmodern fever hangs in the air...

Soviet dissidents risked their lives to print, read, and pass around banned books. Why would they do this? Solzhenitsyn says they did this because great art provides profoundly useful warnings. Cultures "continually repeat each other's mistakes with a time lag." An idea that is tried and rejected in one place emerges in another as the "latest word." Here, art can tide over "differences in language, custom, and social structures" and provide a warning.

Even as the world was obsessed with the Cold War, Solzhenitsyn said "the split in the world is less terrifying than the similarity of the disease afflicting its main sections." We are all headed toward the same cliff. The whole world is defaulting to the same value set, which means one error in this value set can doom the whole planet. Nations should remain differentiated, Solzhenitsyn thought, so the failure of one nation does not cascade globally. And let's not forget how boring things would get if all the differences between different cultures and countries were flattened: "The disappearance of nations would impoverish us no less than if all peoples were made alike, with one character, one face."

Solzhenitsyn notes the insidious relationship between the ease of the modern world, and the weakness of modern men. He says strength only develops via encounters with adversity: "Even biology knows that habitual extreme safety and well-being are not advantageous for a living organism." Contemporary life cranks up comfort at the cost of growth.

39

HOW THE CAT BECAME AN
ICONIC EGYPTIAN SYMBOL

Sexual Personae, 1991

In Ancient Egypt, cats were fed royal diets, adorned with jewels, and considered the vessel of Gods. Upon death, they were often mummified. Camille Paglia explains why:

Paglia believes that each civilization is a new attempt at balancing nature with society. Paglia calls the social order *Apollonian,* and the chaos of nature *Dionysian.* We need the raw materials of nature but also need to survive her tantrums when she's "throwing her weight around."

The Egyptians venerated cats as they are a near-perfect balance between Apollo—the God of order and Dionysus—the deity of chaos. Cats have a sense of beauty and proportion—Apollonian traits. But they love to be unpredictably aggressive—like Dionysian nature herself.

Cats mirror nature: "They live by and for fear, practicing being scared or spooking humans by sudden rushings and ambushes." Cats sleep "up to twenty of every twenty-four hours," moving in a dream world where Apollonian logic is not welcome.

The cat combines its Dionysian love of the dark with its Apollonian love of the spotlight: "But it also fashionably loves to see and be seen; it is a spectator of life's drama, amused, condescending." When ignored, it interrupts your activities with great pomp, getting attention.

Cats also seem to have an apollonian aesthetic sense: "When it is disheveled, its spirits fall. Cats have a sense of pictorial composition: they station themselves symmetrically on chairs, rugs, even a sheet of paper on the floor. Cats adhere to an Apollonian metric of mathematical space."

The Egyptians honored crocodiles for the same reason they worshiped cats: the crocodile inhabits two worlds. The croc undertakes a "daily passage between two realms"—moving between "water and earth." It's equally at ease with the orderly gravity of land and the watery underworld.

There's a logic behind the Christian dislike of cats: "In the Middle Ages, they were hunted and killed for their association with witches." For Paglia, Christianity is an Apollonian enterprise seeking cosmic order—a project at odds with the cat's innate Dionysian energy.

Cats resonated with the Egyptian *spirit* because cats embody a fusion of the Apollonian and Dionysian energies. Paglia writes: "Through the cat, Egypt defined

and refined its complex aesthetic." Cats showed Egypt
that a "unique synthesis" of two warring principles was
possible.

40

HOW TO BE HONORABLE

A soldier kills for a living. Soldiers tend to be "irrational" men with at least a moderate bloodlust. And yet soldiers are considered more *honorable* than merchants. Why's this? The merchants are "peaceable," "rational," and kill no one! John Ruskin, a victorian English polymath, offers a good solution to the mystery of honor:

The soldier's actual profession is not to kill but to die. Ruskin: "Reckless he may be, fond of pleasure or of adventure...But put him in a fortress breach, with all the pleasures of the world behind him, and only death and his duty in front, he will keep his face to the front." The soldier is more honorable because under some conditions, he's willing to die.

Honor is the willingness to die for your land, your principles, your people, or a mix of the three.

Ruskin writes that there are "five great professions" in all societies: "The Soldier's profession is to *defend* it. The Pastor's to *teach* it. The Physician's to keep it in *health*. The Lawyer's to enforce *justice* in it. The

Merchant's to *provide* for it." And on "due occasion," to "die for it."

The soldier must choose death instead of leaving "his post in battle," the physician can't "leave his post in plague" no matter what, the pastor should refuse to speak "falsehoods" come what may. The lawyer must risk his death instead of defending "injustice." And the merchant? What is a Merchant's "due occasion" for death? Ruskin: "For, truly, the man who does not know when to die, does not know how to live."

Ruskin writes a merchant's duty is to use his "sagacity and energy" to produce quality goods available at a cheap price to everyone. Since manufacturing involves the "agency of many lives and hands," a merchant by design is a *leader* of men and must bear "responsibility for the kind of life they lead." A merchant must choose "distress, poverty, or labor" over letting his product deteriorate. He must use all his "intelligence, patience, kindness, tact, and energy" to do his best work.

Just like a captain is the last to leave the ship "in case of a wreck," and a father will give the last breadcrust to the son "in case of famine," a merchant must absorb misfortune and "take more of it for himself than he allows his men to feel." This is what honor demands.

A king that rides into battle with his men, and a merchant that takes on losses and material blows before letting his people get scratched, will inspire a devoted, even a fanatical, loyalty.

Final takeaway: Find things you want to take risk for, work hard for, and die for. But it's important that the feeling be authentic. You must consider the things you're sacrificing for, *sacrifice worthy.*

41

HOW SPEECH HELPED HUMANS CONQUER THE WORLD

The Human Beast, 2006

Every year, since 1972, a public intellectual is invited to deliver the **Jefferson Lecture in Humanities**. Thinkers who can "communicate the knowledge and wisdom of the humanities in a broadly appealing way" are selected. In 2006, the lecturer was Tom Wolfe. He made a fascinating argument that natural selection stopped being relevant to human evolution "11,000 years" ago. Dig in:

Wolfe's central idea: we are no longer homo sapiens but "Homo Loquax," that is, "man talking." Natural selection via the natural environment was overrun and overpowered via the "artificial selection" by culture the moment humans developed speech.

Wolfe on Speech: "It gave the human beast the powers of reason, complex memory, and long-term planning." Without speech, new ideas and technology couldn't break out of one person's mind or life. Speech allowed ideas and technology to spread, which birthed civilization.

Our environment used to shape and select us, now we shape and select our environment. Wolfe: "Speech gave him the power to enlarge his food supply at will through an artifice called farming."

Speech—and the culture that emerges from it—radically upended not just our evolution, but also "the evolution of animals." We're so powerful that we are "sentimental about predators," and help save wild cats from evolutionary extinction.

Natural forces still give us the raw materials, but culture has the final word on what shape they take on. Tom Wolfe: "To say that evolution explains the nature of modern man is like saying that the Bessemer process of adding carbons to pig iron to make steel explains the nature of the modern skyscraper."

Note the *first* verse of the New Testament: "In the beginning was the Word, and the Word was with God, and the Word was God." With speech, we started asking existential questions; that led to religion. Wolfe: "One of Homo loquax's first creations after he learned to talk was religion."

With speech, humans obtained a cultural tool with which they could shape their world faster than their world could shape them.

Wolfe's strong claim that evolution "has been irrelevant for 11,000 years" may be false. But his central idea that speech sets humans apart rings true. Religion, higher culture, and technology all trace their origin to the unique human ability to transmit information and stories.

42

THE DARK SIDE OF EQUALITY

Democracy in America, 1835

When the King of France was put on trial by the revolutionaries, his friends deserted him. One man stood up to defend him: Tocqueville's great-grandfather, Malesherbes. The king was beheaded, and soon after, so was Malesherbes and most of his family. This brutal violence, in the name of a progressive political cause, haunted Tocqueville all his life.

Decades later, Tocqueville crossed the sea, toured the new world and wrote a classic still taught at colleges: Democracy in America. One of the book's big themes is the dark side of equality. Dig in:

The human lust for equality overpowers our love for freedom: "Democratic communities have a natural taste for freedom. But for equality, their passion is insatiable: they call for equality in freedom; and if they cannot obtain that, they still call for equality in slavery."

Democracy is mid: "If a democratic society displays less brilliance than an aristocracy, there will also be less wretchedness; the sciences will be on a smaller scale but ignorance will be less common; you will notice more vices and fewer crimes."

Democracy is a force of atomization: It disconnects us not just from our "ancestors" but also our descendants *and* peers. Tocqueville: "Each man is forever thrown back on himself alone, and there is danger that he may be shut up in the solitude of his own heart." Each man forever thrown back on himself...haunting.

Tocqueville on why you can only let people free IF they're religious: "Despotism may govern without faith, but liberty cannot." Political rules can only be relaxed if moral rules are "strengthened." People can only be "their own masters" once they're "submissive to the Deity."

Safety becomes a big priority in democracies, but safetyism stifles greatness. Bureaucrats and managers cover "society with a network of small, complicated rules, minute and uniform." In such a world, the "most original minds and the most energetic characters" cannot thrive.

Tocqueville on safetyism becoming the organizing principle of life: "What good does it do me if an ever-watchful authority keeps an eye out to ensure that my pleasures will be tranquil and races ahead of me to ward off all danger, sparing me the need even to think?"

In democracies, competing ideologies split people up into rival groups. But a society needs a shared worldview if it is to exist in the long-term: "Without common ideas, there is no common action, and without common action men still exist, but a social body does not." Social action is only possible if the society is bound by "some principle ideas."

Life today punctures a thousand small holes in us, saps our initiative, makes great tasks impossible: "What chiefly diverts the men of democracies from lofty ambition is not the scantiness of their fortunes, but the vehemence of the exertions they daily make to improve them."

It is to the government's advantage if more men of action can be spiritually castrated and turned into NPCs. This is why the state "extinguishes and stupefies" our energies. Tocqueville: "The men are seldom forced to act, but they are constantly restrained from acting."

Tocqueville laments how people are served pre-packaged opinions to swallow in mass democracies: "The majority undertakes to supply a multitude of ready-made opinions for the use of individuals, who are thus relieved from the necessity of forming opinions of their own."

PART FOUR

D FOR DEBATABLE

43

TIME FOR THE BUTLERIAN JIHAD?

Erewhon, 1872

Humans fight a holy war against thinking machines in Dune. This war is called the *Butlerian Jihad*. Why? The war is named after a real 19th century English author: Samuel Butler. Butler issued prophetic warnings against technology in his 1872 novel. His disturbing insights:

A *Dune* prequel tells us that in the future, humans let "efficient machines" execute almost all "everyday tasks." Machines that were meant to save labor and time start eroding our humanity: "Gradually, humans ceased to think, or dream... or truly live." This is the danger of outsourcing life.

Samuel Butler was obsessed with a question: "What sort of creature" will follow us as the ruler of Earth? Life went from minerals to plants to animals—who says we're the ultimate culmination of this process? No rational basis to say "animal life is the end of all things."

In 1863, Butler foresaw machines surpassing us in productivity: "The machine is brisk and active, when the man is weary; it is clear-headed and collected, when the man is stupid and dull; it needs no slumber, when man must sleep or drop; ever at its post, ever ready for work."

Butler saw that our daily lives would get fused with machines. He saw the metaverse coming: "How many men at this hour are living in a state of bondage to the machines?" Today we need everything artificially modified: from the air in our rooms to the images entering our eyes.

Perhaps machines can't be supreme over humans as they can't adapt on the fly. But then, even animals aren't infinitely adaptable: "For how many emergencies is an oyster adapted? For as many as are likely to happen to it, and no more. So are the machines; and so is man himself."

Withdrawing tech of the last 200 years won't just take us back to 1824. An unprecedented war will break out over everything—energy, food, water, space. The world will be much worse than it was in 1824 because of all the technological crutches we need to survive today.

Human dependence will only get worse in the future. Machines will only get more powerful. Today screens give children fake recreations; porn makes real intimacy less likely by flooding us with the artificial.

As the real world slips from our hands, we find solace in fake worlds, from video games to theme parks. When humans win the Butlerian Jihad in Dune, they make a strict commandment: "Thou shalt not disfigure the soul." This is what's at stake: the destiny of our soul.

It's tempting to give into the technological crutches. To just enter the Matrix already. After all, won't it reduce pain and friction? Won't it, on average, be more tolerable than the sweaty, boring, inconvenient, uneventful reality we currently inhabit? Yes, of course. But you will be powerless. Power, mastery over the elements, control...these things are only real in *this* world. And so here we must remain.

44

ALDOUS HUXLEY WANTS YOU TO DELETE NETFLIX

Pleasures, 1920

Aldous Huxley predicted the degeneracy of modern amusements in a 103 year old essay. He said the future man would become weak, stupid, and empty of vitality because of the way he spends his leisure time. Here's Huxley on why and how you need to radically rewire the way you spend your free time:

Aldous Huxley writes that pleasures must not be an escape from effort. In fact, they must be unavailable *without* effort. Why? Because when preceded by effort, pleasure reinvigorates. But when preceded by nothing, pleasure retards your brain's reward systems.

"Entertainment" has regressed. At royal weddings, theological debates were arranged as entertainment. Logicians debated God at Prince Palatine's engagement. Huxley: "There was a time when people indulged themselves with distractions requiring a certain intellectual effort."

Huxley notes that in Elizabethan times, regular people "could be relied upon" to break into complex musical acts like madrigals or motets. People had to "exert their minds to an uncommon degree" to entertain themselves. This kept their minds *supple*. The average person today knows no dance form, no musical instrument...our fingertips move in a frenzy while the rest of our body languishes.

Aldous Huxley hated mass manufactured distractions. On movies: "Countless audiences passively soak in the tepid bath of nonsense. No mental effort is demanded of them, no participation; they need only sit and keep their eyes open." But mental effort is *necessary*.

Huxley writes that in the past, entertainment was a consequence of *active* collaboration between friends, family, and neighbors. Today, these very people sit in darkness in movie theaters and silently watch something that *strangers* made halfway across the world...

In *The World Until Yesterday,* Jared Diamond writes about African kids who make model airplanes from sticks and stones by looking at a newspaper picture. Kids in rich societies buy airplane sets from the mall. Kids' entertainment becomes passive in advanced societies...

Huxley on how tech makes us LESS creative: "Before machinery men who wanted to amuse themselves were compelled, in their humble way, to be artists. Now they sit still and permit professionals to entertain them with machinery." "Artistic culture" dies in such an environment...

In Huxley's Brave New World, the "savage" says the following to the technocrat who wants humanity happy and comfortable: "But I don't want comfort. I want God, I want poetry, I want real danger, I want freedom, I want goodness, I want sin." These are conditions for GROWTH.

Notice the "fort" in comfort. The Latin root of comfort means to *fortify*—to make stronger. The original sense of comfort was rest that *readies* you for war. *Not* lounging without aim. Aldous Huxley writes that we must return to the original meaning of the word...

45

A TIMELESS DEFENSE OF FAITH

The Will To Believe, 1896

We moderns think faith is backward and low-status. To crunch big data and make evidence-based decisions—that is the height of progressive sophistication. But more than a 100 years ago, William James, one of the founding fathers of psychology, argued that we will *fail* in our attempt to flee from faith. In a lecture called **The Will To Believe**, he put up a timeless defense of faith:

William James asks: Is our tendency to find and stick by dogmas something we "must free ourselves" from, or something we must stand by—even "endorse"? The latter, he answers.

Science styles itself as the great enemy of faith, but it's *premised* on an unprovable faith: "Our belief that there is a truth, and that our minds and it are made for each other—what is it but a passionate desire?" And let's not forget that science often progresses thanks to "the passionate desires of individuals to get their own faiths confirmed."

We are more than algorithms who decide—who are animals who must act. And to act, we must choose between options—often on the basis of an instinct, hunch or faith. We live in an uncertain world in which we must nevertheless act, and faith is our friend in such a world.

The human condition is to choose, act, and move through life without having certain knowledge in advance. William James asks: "Objective evidence and certitude are doubtless very fine ideals to play with, but where on this moonlit and dream-visited planet are they found?" This is a moonlit and dream-visited planet, not one bleached with the fluorescent glow of total knowledge.

Moral questions are too urgent and important to be left to science: "Moral questions present themselves as questions whose solution can't wait for sensible proof. A moral question is a question not of what sensibly exists, but of what is good, or would be good if it *did* exist."

The rational mind waits for verification before having faith, but faith sometimes brings its own verification: "Who gains promotions, boons, appointments, but the man who sacrifices other things for their sake before they have come, and takes risks for them in advance?" There are cases where "a fact cannot come at all unless a preliminary faith exists in its coming."

Reality is not an untouchable and unshakeable thing that can only be studied—it's a dynamic drama where our *decisions* sway the result, and our *faith* sways our decisions.

Faith can never be completely erased—even from a single human mind—because in all significant moments of life, James writes, "we have to take a leap in the dark." Everyone is fated to find a fork in the road where the choice is not between evidence and faith, but two faiths.

46

THE MARK OF A FIRST-RATE INTELLIGENCE IS...

The Great Gatsby author Scott Fitzgerald wrote in 1936:

"The test of a first-rate intelligence is the ability to hold two opposed ideas in the mind at the same time, and still retain the ability to function. One should, for example, be able to see that things are hopeless and yet be determined to make them otherwise." When two things contradict each other yet appear to be simultaneously true, you may have chanced upon a third greater truth.

Here are ten interesting paradoxes to stretch your brain.

The Paradox of Logic. Napoleon said logic will lose you wars because sometimes the moment demands imaginative maneuvers that work *because* they are irrational.

The Paradox of Beauty. Chateaubriand said beauty is useless if you care for efficiency, but shockingly useful if you care for lovability. Yes, beauty is a wasteful luxury but ultimately the only thing people will protect, and make pilgrimages to.

The Paradox of Time. La Rochefoucauld: "Absence diminishes small loves and increases great ones, as the wind blows out the candle and fans the bonfire." Time will kill everything shallow, and deepen everything real.

The Paradox of Originality. C.S. Lewis said originality is best attained via copying. Exposure to past masterworks will spark off novel ideas. But close yourself off to all inspiration from others, all admiration of the greats, all lessons from the past, and you will ironically produce something dull and nonsensical.

The Paradox of Compassion. The road to hell is paved with compassion. Nietzsche argued compassion is a psyop designed by the weak to redirect resources from the most deserving to the least. Communist revolutions start in the name of compassion and end with all the competent people murdered, and all the inept ones in power. Compassion feels sweet but there's no bitterer aftertaste.

The Paradox of Hate. Chesterton: "You need to hate the world enough to change it, but love it enough to consider it worth changing." Action is the offspring of dark pessimism and frenzied optimism...working in tandem.

The Paradox of Liberalism. Camille Paglia: "Liberalism defines government as tyrant father but demands it behave as nurturant mother." Society must be so tyrannical that you should be protected from mean tweets but also so permissive that you should be able to change your gender (and back).

The Paradox of Great Writing. John Morley said Great writing dances at the border of mysterious and obvious. Too mysterious and you're inaccessible, too obvious and you're boring.

The Paradox of Democracy. Julius Evola said democracy has hurt the demos (people) the most by disempowering their natural superiors. Evola: "It is not the superior who has need of the inferior, but the inferior who has need of the superior; it is not the master that has need of the minion, it is the minion that has need of a master."

The Paradox of High IQ. John Fowles: High IQ is a terrifying gift. The ability to predict the consequences of any action means your will gets lost in a "labyrinth of hypotheses." Rule 1: Do not lose the will.

47

GOD IS DEAD. NOW WHAT?

The Gay Science, 1882

"God is dead" is modern philosophy's boldest and the most misunderstood statement. Contemporary atheism takes it to be a triumphant and celebratory announcement, but for Nietzsche it was a great tragedy. Here's a breakdown of what Nietzsche meant:

In The Gay Science, Nietzsche announced God's death for the first time. For Nietzsche, God was not a drag on progress, the "opium of the masses," or an irrational filter that distorted our view of reality. What was God, then? Let's look at the metaphors Nietzsche uses for God.

God as Sun. The sun holds the planets in their orbit; similarly God oriented us. Now, with the death of God, we are unchained from our sun. Nietzsche: "Are we not plunging continually? Backward, sideward, forward, in all directions?" Our center of gravity is gone—we're hurtling through "an infinite nothing."

God as horizon. Nietzsche asks: "Who gave us the sponge to wipe away the entire horizon?" The horizon keeps sailors on track when at sea. The horizon provides direction and holds the promise of ports to dock at. With the horizon wiped off, where do we look to in stormy seas?

God as light. The madman who announces God's death is carrying a lit lantern in broad daylight. Without God, we must carry our personal fragile flames now. Illumination is no longer a *given*.

Who killed God? We did. This task was " too great for us." Nietzsche asks: "What water is there for us to clean ourselves? What festivals of atonement, what sacred games shall we have to invent?" Our cosmic father is dead, and we are now orphans in a hostile universe. Nietzsche wonders if we must now "become gods" simply to justify what we did.

The profound implications of God's death will unfold over centuries. Our faith in God's existence underpinned a lot of what we take for granted—doesn't the idea of human rights and universal equality come from the notion of *each created in God's image?*

Faith in God was the invisible foundation for much of civilization; all of this is now on shaky ground. We will need new justifications, new fixed horizons, new sources of illumination, and new reliable centers of gravity. Who's creative enough to create all of this from scratch?

Bottomline. Nietzsche: "God is dead. God *remains* dead." Now who, or what, can do God's job? The tasks done by even the *concept* of God are too numerous for a simple conceptual replacement. God's death has left a void; to even begin to fill it requires great daring and creativity.

48

HOW WARS ARE FOUGHT FOR
MONEY NOT PRINCIPLES

War Is A Racket, 1931

Smedley Butler became the most decorated Marine in U.S. history. He won battles on 3 continents. Yet he wasn't proud of his work...he called himself a "gangster for capitalism." After 34 years, he retired to deliver an infamous speech. Here are insights the world must remember:

A racket is an enterprise whose hidden purpose is only known to a select few. Butler: "It is conducted for the benefit of the very few, at the expense of the very many." War perfectly fits this definition—millions are maimed or killed so a few thousand can make untold fortune.

Wars are waged not for democracy or peace, but for the business interests who profit wildly during war time. The young men who kill and die aren't told the real reason they're being marched off. Instead they're shamed into it.

Psychological manipulation and lies are used to fool soldiers into signing up and fighting. Clergymen say the war is ordained by God himself—young men are shamed if they don't "join the army." WW1 was marketed as the "war to end all wars"—yet WW2 happened 20 years later.

Who profits from war, exactly? Butler lists them: "Munitions makers. Bankers. Ship builders. Manufacturers. Meat packers. Speculators." War supercharges the profits of certain industries, as their products are now demanded and bought by the ultimate spender: a wartime government.

There's no overlap between those who fight the war—and those who profit from it. Butler reported that "21,000 new millionaires and billionaires" were minted during WW1. He asked: "How many of them dug a trench? How many of them went hungry in a rat-infested dug-out?"

Du Ponts manufactured gunpowder, and saw their profits jump by "more than 950%" in WW-I. Or take the Leather Company—they saw "a small increase of 1,100%."

20 million mosquito nets were sold to the U.S. government in WW1: "I suppose the boys were expected to put it over them as they tried to sleep in muddy trenches—one hand scratching cooties on their backs and the other making passes at scurrying rats." The nets never reached the warfront.

The shoe manufacturers love war as it brings "business with abnormal profits." They sold the US government 35 million pairs of shoes in WW1—General Butler writes his regiment had "only one pair" per soldier. At the end of the war, 25 million pairs were left unused.

The shipbuilders built and sold $635 million worth of wooden ships to the US government that "wouldn't float." General Butler: "The seams opened up -- and they sank. We paid for them, though. And somebody pocketed the profits." The US government spent a billion dollars on "building airplane engines that never left the ground!"

And the men on the front? Those soldiers often got no money on "payday." They paid for their own "accident insurance." They had to fund their own "ammunition, clothing, and food" through compulsory "liberty bonds." When the pay day came, most soldiers got nothing in hand.

The US army was convinced by some businessmen that "colonels shouldn't ride in automobiles, nor should they even ride on horseback." 6,000+ buckboards—four wheeled carriages driven by a large animal—were sold to the government "for the use of colonels!" Never used.

War takes normal men and turns them into killers. Butler saw how men were taken out of "fields and offices and classrooms" and trained to become very good at mass murder. When the war was over, they were "discharged" and told to become normal again—a reversal impossible for many.

The psychological damage of war is hard to quantify. War gives young men "tremendous excitement"—when the survivors return, they're suddenly cut off from it. These extreme swings drive some of them insane. Butler saw many veterans of WW1 in government hospitals—they were "mentally destroyed."

To end the war racket, those who profit from the war must be sent to the frontlines. Before anyone else, "the directors and the high-powered executives of the armament factories" must be sent to fight. Bankers who profit from the war must be "conscripted."

Secondly, those who will be called upon to fight, kill, and die should vote upon the war. Butler: "Only those who would be called upon to risk their lives for their country should have the privilege of voting to determine whether the nation should go to war."

49

WHEN EXPERTS GO WRONG

Psychological Care Of Infant and Child, 1928

Meet John Watson: the father of Behaviorism. In 1928, he wrote a parenting guide. It became a best-seller. Then his kids started killing themselves. Here's a story of scientific arrogance, the meaning of love, and one expert who was very, very wrong...

Dr. John Watson was a man of bold claims. He believed he could turn a random infant into "any type of specialist" from doctor to artist to a thief—"regardless of his talents, tendencies, abilities." How? With psychological conditioning and other tools of behaviorism.

John Watson shared these tools with the world in a book he co-wrote with his wife. "Society" comes up 8 times in the book. The "environment" comes up 10 times. But "soul" comes up 0 times. Among other things, the book says a mother's love is "dangerous."

Watson taught millions that giving kids love without reason sets up bad incentives. The world doesn't comfort a person for crying, so neither should a mother. Parents must be "objective" and "free from sentiment." Watson walked his talk. Let's check in on his kids...

Years after Watson's death, his son gave a tell-all interview: "We were never shown any kind of emotional closeness. It was absolutely verboten in the family." Getting close to parents was "taboo." Watson had 4 kids, and 3 of them, from 2 different marriages, tried suicide. One succeeded.

Watson's wife had doubts about her famous husband's "wisdom." She once revealed her "secret wish"—that "her sons have a tear in their eyes for the poetry and drama of life and a throb for romance." BUT in practice she toe'd her husband's line even when he "wasn't looking."

Watson's son: "My reason for entering therapy was an attempted suicide. I strongly believe that strict adherence to the principles of behaviorism tends to erode the fundamental development of the child's ego strength and to cause a great deal of difficulty in later life."

Watson's kids were never allowed to switch on the "night lights" no matter the thunder storms outside. They weren't allowed toys either. Their sex ed started at 7. They would later find out that their father always "slept with the light on because of his own dread of the dark."

Watson's blindspot is the blindspot of modernity. Above all he cared about "independence" and "non involvement." He believed kids shouldn't "know their own parents" and could be better brought up in communal homes. Today the world suffers from this atomized vision of humanity.

For Watson, love was unearned validation that promoted mediocrity. But love is actually unearned faith, and faith is ALWAYS unearned. To be loved is to have someone presuppose value and latent greatness in you without proof—the foundation of self-esteem. As Chesterton said: "Men did not love Rome because she was great. She was great because they had loved her."

50

10 CONCEPTS (FROM ANCIENT ROME) THAT EXPLAIN THE MODERN WORLD

1. **The Tacitus Razor:** "If you want to know who controls you, see who you're not allowed to criticize." Hence comedians are the canaries in the coalmine—they go around calling everyone naked, and soon discover who the emperor is.

2. **The Slavery Syndrome:** Sallust: "Few men desire liberty; most men wish only for a just master." Genuine liberty means making decisions 24/7; parsing right from wrong; solving pesky dilemmas using nothing but one's own mind. Liberty is thus too cognitively taxiing for most...people would rather outsource their agency.

3. **The Polybius Warning:** 2nd century B.C. historian Polybius warned that a falling birth

precedes civilizational collapse. Fewer births mean men and women are disinterested in the future. Sloth grows, spiritual concerns are replaced by material ones, and population falls. Social downfall is never too far. Polybius believed the Greek civilization fell due to its "low birth rate..."

4. **The Pliny Principle:** Rene Descartes pinned bodily existence onto the mind—"I think, therefore I am"—but Ancient Rome's magistrate Pliny the Younger said it was the other way around: "It is wonderful how the mind is stirred and quickened into activity by brisk bodily exercise." Only physical exertion leads to healthy mental activity...

5. **The Vitruvius Rule:** Modern architects love asymmetric buildings, but Ancient Roman architect Vitruvius said a building out of proportions is like a deformed body. Nature herself "composed the human body" and the rest of creation using "due proportions." The Vitruvius Rule: No symmetry, off to cemetery.

6. **The Tyranny of Laws:** More laws doesn't mean a more just society. Tacitus: "The more numerous the laws, the more corrupt the government." Make a million laws and you can catch anyone for anything, anytime you want.

7. **The Cassius Hypothesis:** Historian Cassius wrote that while Monarchy needed only one man to make the right decisions, democracy needed millions. Which one is likely to succeed? No wonder, Cassius wrote, that "successes have always been greater and more frequent under kings than under popular rule..."

8. **The Livy Effect:** Historian Livy lived through the Roman civil war and discovered the butterfly effect 20 centuries before the chaos theorists: "Events of great consequence often spring from trifling circumstances." Politics, economics, human acts, ideas...they form one giant mesh of life, and tiny acts can and do snowball.

9. **Greed is Good?** Crassus, the richest man in Rome and part of the First Triumvirate with Pompey and Caesar, said: "Greed is but a word jealous men inflict upon the ambitious." The

animals are ungreedy and stop at their daily meal. Man is anxious, restless, greedy...and master of all known realms. To the unsatisfied and the insatiable we owe everything.

10. **The Juvenal Principle:** "Give them bread and circuses and they will never revolt." Roman poet Juvenal believed a "long peace" was as evil as a war. The modern world needs to rediscover his warning against luxury—to let "bread and circuses" sedate us into action is to betray our very soul.

51

WHY EDUCATION WILL ALWAYS BE DOGMATIC

What's Wrong With the World? 1910

What is the purpose of education?

A current year citizen thinks for a minute and responds: to churn out curious citizens. That's a terrible answer, G.K. argues. An education that teaches kids to be curious about everything and judge nothing is failing at its central task. Chesterton argues it's impossible to separate education from the question of *values*. Education can't be neutral—the very purpose of education is to help kids tell *good* from *bad*. Let's dig in.

Education is not an absolute good, like truth or beauty. Chesterton: "Education is a word like transmission or inheritance; it is not an object, but a method." Education in and itself is neither beneficial nor harmful. To educate is to pass on knowledge and lessons to kids—it's the *content* of the lessons that is key.

Education versus Dogma: " It is quaint that people talk of separating dogma from education. Dogma is actually the only thing that cannot be separated from education. It is education. A teacher who is not dogmatic is simply a teacher who is not teaching."

In the classroom, certain things must be shown to be more important than others. Chesterton: "Mr. Bernard Shaw once said that he hated the idea of forming a child's mind. In that case Mr. Bernard Shaw had better hang himself; for he hates something inseparable from human life."

Education is never without "intellectual violence." It involves encouraging certain faculties while repressing certain tendencies. Education must shape a human being like a sculptor shapes his stones into breathtaking artwork—but that involves chopping, chipping, cutting.

Chesterton: "Education is violent; because it is creative. It is creative because it is human. It's as reckless as playing on the fiddle; as dogmatic as drawing a picture; as brutal as building a house. In short, it is what all human action is: an interference with life and growth."

We have a "high audacious duty" to share truths with the next generation with an "unshaken voice." Modern moral relativism takes flight from this responsibility. We must find absolute truths—if we don't, we are shrinking from an "awful and ancestral responsibility."

Instead of eternal truths, kids today are taught fads: "It ought to be the oldest things that are taught to the youngest people; the assured and experienced truths that are put first to the baby. But in a school today the baby has to submit to a system that is younger than himself."

Bottom line. Education is theological because it's impossible to teach good without first deciding *what* is good, impossible to warn against the bad without determining what it is. Our heavy burden is to put morality on firm ground lest we leave a moral quicksand for posterity.

52

THE MYSTERY OF LANGUAGE

Virtue Signaling, 2019

Thousands of animals can run, hunt, see, smell, hear...but humans are the only ones who can use language. Why, and how, did we evolve this unique ability? Geoffrey Miller, an evolutionary psychologist, explains in his essay, *Why Bother To Speak*:

Perhaps language evolved because it benefits tribes, and humans are tribal. A group whose members talk can circulate warnings and other information faster. But for a trait or behavior to stick around, it must be beneficial for the *individual* too. And from the individual's perspective, talking looks "costly." Miller: "Most animals keep their knowledge, quite selfishly, to themselves. This makes human language look puzzling from a Darwinian viewpoint. Why do we bother to say anything remotely true, interesting, or relevant to anybody who is not closely related to us?" Telling "useful things" to non-relatives could help their genes at the expense of your own.

Miller considers primatologist Robin Dunbar's argument. Dunbar tried to solve the "altruism problem" of speaking by arguing that language is akin to primate grooming. Other apes earn social capital by *grooming* each other for hours; humans earn it by *gossiping* for hours. Miller then poses a challenge: "If language is just verbal grooming, why is it about anything?"

In other words, why does language have any *meaning*? It could've just been a simple set of grunts, huffs, moans and hums.

Next, Miller considers the argument of linguist Robbins Burling. Burling points out that men with public speaking skills are rewarded with high status, and this directly translates to reproductive success. Perhaps language games evolved as a sophisticated *variant* of an activity that's as old as time: male dick measuring contests.

But this explanation, Miller writes cheekily, "doesn't explain why women talk too."

Here's how Geoffrey Miller explains the mystery of language. Humans learnt to talk—and it became a skill equally shared by both the sexes, unless, say, the ability to do pushups— because of "sexual selection." Miller: "Language evolved because our ancestors favored sexual partners who could show off what they knew, remembered, and imagined."

Miller argues humans use language as a *proxy* for intelligence. Speaking well suggests the speaker can observe the world, collect his thoughts, and express them properly. It reveals social skills. Therefore we judge potential mates by, among other things, how well they speak.

In his book *The Mating Mind (1999)*, Miller argues that the human brain is not just a survival machine—it is also a "courtship machine." To ensure their genetic success, our ancestors didn't just have to survive in the day—they also had to seduce at night. Perhaps "the mind evolved by moonlight." And so did conversing skills.

Language made possible different arts like theater, lyrical songs, and stories. The arts themselves have a deep "evolutionary purpose." We know that because arts are universal (stuff that provides an evolutionary edge spreads *universally*), they give pleasure (evolution makes adaptive behaviors pleasurable), and they have huge energy and time costs (Energy and time are never wasted without purpose.)

Miller's final word: "Sexual selection made our brains wasteful: it transformed a small, efficient ape-style brain into a huge, energy hungry handicap spewing out luxury behaviors like conversation, music, and art." The brain's job is to help you survive—but also to get you laid. A smooth tongue goes a long way there.

53

THE ANTI-STOIC MANIFESTO

Stoicism and its consequences have been a disaster for the human race.

When Marcus Aurelius was writing his journals, his wife was cucking him. She was sleeping with gladiators. Marcus went so deep on detachment that he detached from his self-respect too. Not good. Very bad.

"There's such a thing as too much meditation."—Elon Musk.

Reject stoicism. Reject Buddhism. Even the room lizard is "tranquil." Get ATTACHED. Everything great is downstream of (strong) desires. The Latin root for desire is "de sidere," which translates to "from the stars." An intense desire is a gift from the Gods above. A gift of direction.

Nihilism is the number one psychological sickness of our time. And what is nihilism but the inability to desire anything?

The heartbreak of desire unfulfilled is dark and vast, but better a broken heart than a frozen one.

Desire is the engine of life. Without it...stagnation.

The ultimate human fate cannot be to attain the equanimity of sheep grazing out on a sunny day. We are the "upstart species" (Oswald Spengler) and our natural habitat is the edge. Our only habitat. The edge is a hurtful, torturous place but it's the only place we can birth something new.

Nihilism is the ultimate psyop. Nietzsche wrote this on the first page of his last book (1889). A vague sense that nothing really matters. You need to scrub this feeling out of your soul with as much aggression and venom as you can muster. Nihilism is the Meta Problem.

The most powerless creature in the world is not an ant, not the grounded plant, but a nihilist. The ant and the plant will automatically fight to preserve themselves but this central instinct of life has been removed from the nihilist's toolkit. He is compromised beyond saving.

Those who tell you the world is worthless will, after you renounce it, rush in to rule. It's a power grab, plain and simple. This is why for Nietzsche, the way out of nihilism is not community service or "sacrifice" but Will To Power. A healthy controlling urge is the antidote.

A standard movie trope: you only meet the villain's lackeys and side pieces at the beginning. Then there's a grand revelation of the main villain at the end. Nihilism is that main villain, and the movie is human history. He stands unmasked now, and the protagonist must fight.

Nihilism takes on insidious shapes. Here are some. The feeling that you are puny next to deterministic historical forces or climate change or whatever. The feeling that the inside is more worthy of attention than the outside. The sense that your agency is limited. The instinct of surrender to fate. All nihilism. Reject fully.

Nihilism condemns you to a fate worse than that of an insect or a rock. A rock has no dignity to speak of, and even an insect unironically pursues its goals. The sooner you fight and overcome nihilism, the sooner your real life begins. And there is only one way out.

54

H.P. LOVECRAFT SEEKS THE HIGHER LIFE

Nietzscheism and Realism, 1921

H.P. Lovecraft, the famous horrorist who wrote *The Call of Cthulhu*, comes across as a soulful aristocrat in his obscure essays and personal letters. He attacks mass democracy, critiques modern priorities, and describes alternative goals that society must aim at. Dig in:

A great society can only be built when the most gifted contribute. And for their contribution, the aristocrats must be rewarded: "Since the only human motive is a craving for supremacy, we can expect nothing in the way of achievement unless achievement be rewarded by supremacy."

Civilization must create valuable "thoughts and objects" and aristocracy "alone" can do this. Democracies live "parasitically on the aristocracies they overthrow." And over time, democracies use up "the aesthetic and intellectual resources which autocracy bequeathed them."

The difference between aristocracy, democracy, and mob rule: "In an aristocracy some persons have a great deal to live for. In a democracy most persons have a little to live for. In an ochlocracy(mob rule) nobody has anything to live for."

Science and art trickle down from the top: The ultrawealthy turn their surplus capital and attention toward the "full appreciation of beauty and truth." "Most of the pleasures" felt by the average man wouldn't exist if the wealthy didn't use their spare resources to cultural ends.

No aristocracy is permanently protected from democracy; no democracy is permanently protected from ambitious aristocrats. The masses eventually over-run the palaces. And then the aristocrats eventually take advantage of the indifferent, scatter-brained masses to win power back.

Lovecraft doesn't want repressive autocracies: "Moderation is essential in all things."

Lovecraft gives all governments a very simple task: "Government need go no further than to safeguard an aristocratic class in its opulence and dignity so that it may be left free to create the ornaments of life and to attract the ambition of others who seek to rise to it."

Aristocracies can't be closed off: "The healthiest aristocracy is the most elastic – willing to beckon and receive all men of whatever antecedents who prove themselves aesthetically and intellectually fitted for membership." Make the aspirational life available to the deserving.

H.P. Lovecraft explains the difference between real and fake aristocrats: "The real aristocrat is ever reasonable, kindly, and affable toward the masses – it is the incompletely cultured novus homo (new man) who makes ostentation of his power and position."

HP Lovecraft is spiritually opposed to the democratic reformer, the man who is obsessed with the "welfare of the masses." The democrat embraces the "mental-emotional point of view" of the masses and would "willingly sacrifice the finest fruits of civilization for the sake of stuffing their bellies." Lovecraft explains the difference between them: "The reformer cares only for the masses, but may make concessions to the civilization. I care only for civilization, but may make concessions to the masses. Do you not see the antipodal difference?"

Lovecraft wishes to cause no pain. "Deliberate cruelty" towards any form of life is "coarse and unaesthetic." All he cares about is civilization, which for him, is a system of "gratifying the complex mental-emotional-aesthetic needs of highly evolved and acutely sensitive men."

Highly evolved humans need great art, noble adventures, and the freedom to sincerely search for the truth. These needs are only satisfied under the aristocratic conditions of wealth, luxury, high artistic and moral standards, generational missions, and protection from everyday fads.

I love HP Lovecraft's description of the artistic process. The artist first sees something important, good, or beautiful in the world—something invisible to others. Then he uses the mediums he's best acquainted with to bring his vision to the world. Full quote from a letter: "Good art means the ability of any one man to pin down in some permanent and intelligible medium a sort of idea of what he sees in Nature that nobody else sees. In other words, to make the other fellow grasp, through skilled selective care in interpretative reproduction or symbolism, some inkling of what only the artist himself could possibly see in the actual objective scene itself."

Civilization should be set up for the production of beauty and greatness: "We advocate the preservation of conditions favorable to the growth of beautiful things — imposing palaces, beautiful cities, elegant literature, reposeful art and music, and a physically select human type."

PART FIVE

E FOR EUREKA!

55

C.S. LEWIS TAKES YOU ON A BUS RIDE TO HELL

The Great Divorce, 1945

The Great Divorce came to C.S. Lewis in a dream. It's the story of a group of ghosts taking a bus ride from hell to heaven. This book helped me better understand the nature of hell. You don't need to be fully convinced of the *physicality* of hell to talk about it. The reason we should talk about hell is that we cannot act—or even properly *think*—without *some* idea of the ultimate good and the ultimate bad. Thinking of hell is a useful way to wrestle with the nature of absolute evil, and how one might end up there. Let's start:

Describing hell = expanding hell. C.S. Lewis writes the modern "wish to describe Hell" is an attempt to expand hell. Relentless complaining, permanent dissatisfaction, a refusal to ever acknowledge truth or beauty—these are the acts of salesmen of hell.

Where do opinions come from? Lewis asks if our opinions are "honestly come by." More often than not, we absorb—and then project—beliefs only because they seem "modern and successful."

The most terrifying thing about the road to hell is how uneventful and gentle it is. A small compromise, a tiny sin, a fleeting moment of cowardice...repeated over a lifetime...and you're in hell. C.S. Lewis: "The safest road to Hell is the gradual one—the gentle slope, soft underfoot, without sudden turnings, without milestones, without signposts."

Here's how NOT to deal with the past. One of the ghosts in the novel is clinging onto her past. She says: "The past was all I had." But to embalm and freeze the past for eternity—like an Egyptian mummy—is the "wrong way to deal with sorrow."

The spirit of inquiry has been corrupted. The proper way to inquire is to seek answers, not to get addicted to questions. One ghost in *The Great Divorce,* representing the corruption of the scientific spirit, compares endless questions to endless traveling: "To travel hopefully is better than to arrive." But then comes a response: Without a destination, "how could anyone travel hopefully?"

Art has been subverted too. The origin of good art is simple: the artist catches "glimpses of Heaven" somewhere, and puts it down on paper or canvas. But when a love of the medium takes precedence over heavenly inspiration, the artist—and her art—is lost.

Pity is often misused in the modern world. Lewis writes that pity's proper role is to be "a spur that drives joy to help misery." But pity is often wrongly *inverted*. From The Great Divorce: "Those who choose misery can hold joy up to ransom, by pity. " Pity can be the invisible chain the miserable use to control the joyous.

Hell is where the spirit of inquiry is corrupted into endless questioning, where art is without inspiration, and where pity is used as an excuse to spread misery.

Final word from C.S. Lewis: "The doors of hell are locked on the *inside*. I do not mean that the ghosts may not wish to come out of hell, in the vague fashion wherein an envious man 'wishes' to be happy: but they certainly do not will even the first preliminary stages of that self-abandonment through which alone the soul can reach any good. They enjoy forever the horrible freedom they have demanded, and are therefore self-enslaved."

56

THE HELL OF BAD HABITS

The Laws of Habit, 1899

Here's William James on the nature of habits and how to build better ones:

William James describes people as "bundles of habits." The laws of nature themselves are nothing but habits that the material world adheres to. But what, exactly, are habits? James uses an evocative metaphor to answer this question.

Habit as folded paper. Fold a paper once, and folding it over the same crease line will get easier each subsequent time. Habits have this quality: once they set in, they get easier and faster to execute over time.

William James notes the "Law of the Conservation of Direction." Thoughts, actions, and material phenomena keep going just because they "happen to have once begun." Once physic, behavioral, or material patterns set in, the patterns become more entrenched.

Since a habit "simplifies the movements required to achieve a given result," the purpose of habits is clear: to free up our time and energy. A habit "diminishes the fatigue" suffered from executing a certain task.

Automate everything you can and free up your mind. William James on the purpose of education: "To make automatic and habitual, as early as possible, as many useful actions as we can, and to guard against growing into ways that are likely to be disadvantageous."

The most "miserable human being" is the one with no habits. Cognitive real-estate is precious, and mustn't be cluttered with endless deliberation over mundane acts. A person "in whom nothing is habitual but indecision"—who pauses before every move—wastes his life on tedium.

Here's how to fight off, and lift, above the gravity of bad old habits: use enormous initial momentum. William James suggests: "Put yourself assiduously in conditions that encourage the new way; take a public pledge; in short, envelop your resolution with every aid you know."

According to William James, this is THE most important habit to cultivate: "Be systematically ascetic or heroic in little unnecessary points." Get into the habit of doing things you "would rather not do." When real hardship comes, your *instincts* will be ready.

A person without pre-set habits will waste his life on trivial decisions. The right habits preserve attention and energy for better things. Massive initial momentum helps beat the pull of bad habits, and *habitual* asceticism trains our reflexes for real difficulties.

57

THE INVERSION OF SYMBOLS

*Recognitions: Studies on Men from the Perspective of the
Right, 1974*

Julius Evola, an Italian philosopher, wrote that modern
revolutionary movements take "the principles, the forms,
and the traditional symbols" of healthier societies and
give them a corrupt new spin. He gives three examples:
the color red, the word revolution, and the symbol of the
pentagrammic star. Let's dig in:

In his essay The Inversion of Symbols, Evola wrote that
revolutions today don't stand for "something positive" or
give life to "autonomous and original forms." What they
really do is agitate for "usurpation."

Take the color red. In Ancient Rome, the Emperor was
dressed and dyed in purplish Red to "represent Jove, the
King of the Gods." In Catholicism, the "Princes of the
Church," the cardinals, wear a scarlet red robe.
Traditionally, red has been linked with hierarchy, order,
and power.

In "classical antiquity," fire was linked with the color
red, and the "heaven above heaven" was composed of

pure fire. Red stood for authority and hierarchy—but in the 20th century it was co-opted by Marxists and made to represent the opposite idea: equality, masses, and democracy.

The same inversion happened with the word *revolution*. Evola: "Revolution in the primary sense does not mean subversion and revolt, but really even the opposite: return to a point of departure and ordinary motion around a center." In physics this holds true: a star's revolution means "gravitating around a center."

A revolution is what keeps a star in a stable orbit—traditional societies imagined a revolution to be a movement that keeps the moral universe spinning in harmony. But today a revolution means moving away from stable centers, continuous churn, and destruction of regularity.

Evola: "Modern Revolution is like the unhinging of the door, the opposite of the traditional meaning of the term: the social and political forces loosen from their natural orbit, *decline*, no longer know any center or order, other than a badly and temporarily stemmed disorder."

The Pentagram. The pentagram, a 5 pointed star, traditionally stood for man's destiny as the microcosm that contained the macrocosm. It represented man as "the image of the world and of God, dominator of all the elements thanks to his dignity and his supernatural destination."

The star represented man as "spiritually integrated and supernaturally sovereign"—but Marxists took this symbol and changed its meaning. They "terrestrialized and collectivized" it—it went on the flags of the USSR and Communist China, becoming "destructive of every higher value."

Evola: "This degradation of symbols is, for every attentive overview, an extremely significant and eloquent sign of the times." Symbols are the universal visual language. This radical transformation of their meaning is not accidental. They're intentionally retooled for "inversion, subversion, and degradation."

58

A 2,700 YEAR OLD MASTERCLASS ON HUMAN PSYCHOLOGY

Fragments, 6th century B.C.

Heraclitus wrote one single book on a papyrus scroll. He gave up the throne of Ephesus, Greece to his younger brother. Not a single copy of his book survives. But some snippets do live on in the form of quotes in other books. These snippets influenced Plato, Marcus Aurelius, Heidegger and others. Let's dig in:

The moderns are obsessed with how to live, the ancients were obsessed with how to die. Heraclitus: "The luckiest men die worthwhile deaths." What is a worthwhile death is every man's individual puzzle to solve. But perhaps honor, courage, and principles are part of the answer...

Heraclitus on why we need a break from rules: "The rule that makes its subject weary is a sentence of hard labor. For this reason, change gives rest." When we get stuck in the same pattern, life feels like clockwork. We feel like automated bots. Then we seek a break in the pattern.

Heraclitus on the importance of conflict: "The poet was a fool who wanted no conflict among us, Gods or people.

Harmony needs low and high, as progeny needs man and woman." Life is only possible in the tension between opposites. Our world's strife is what makes it fertile.

Heraclitus on why failing is good: "Always having what we want may not be the best good fortune. Health seems sweetest after sickness, food in hunger, goodness in the wake of evil, and at the end of daylong labor sleep." It's GOOD to lose, to suffer, if only to feel the contrast.

Heraclitus on how the masses get manipulated in democracies: "What use are these people's wits, who let themselves be led by speechmakers, in crowds, without considering how many fools and thieves they are among, and how few choose the good?" Even people with wits are misled by propaganda.

On dreams, Heraclitus was twenty centuries ahead of everyone: "Even a soul submerged in sleep is hard at work, and helps make something of the world." We now understand that dreams help with coherence construction—Heraclitus knew they "help make something of the world."

Heraclitus on how to live: "The best choose progress toward one thing, a name forever honored by the gods, while others eat their way toward sleep like nameless oxen." What is this "one thing," a name forever "honored" by the Gods? Perhaps he means goals of enduring value: excellence, power, and true loyalty.

Heraclitus a century before Socrates: "All people ought to know themselves." Heraclitus was onto meditation, journaling, and self-reflection in 5th century BC: "Applicants for wisdom do what I've done: inquire within." But also note he was known as the weeping philosopher...

Let's finish with Heraclitus' most iconic quote: "No man ever steps into the same river twice." There is no freeze frame in nature. You cannot go to the same place twice as it has changed since you last saw it. You cannot kiss the same woman twice as in-between breaths, she has transformed ever so imperceptibly. You can't read the same book again because now you are different. Flux is all.

59

THE PSYCHOLOGY OF SETTLING

FOR LESS

The Nobel Prize in Economics, 1978 Banquet Speech

In 1978, for the first time in history, a *non-economist* won the Nobel Prize For Economics. He was Herbert Simon, a political scientist. He landed the Nobel Prize for overturning the three big assumptions of classical economics. Let's see what they are.

Classical economics assumes people are *rational* actors with *unlimited* resources and ultimate time to search for the *optimum* solution. There are three errors here..

Error one: A person's rationality isn't boundless. People have biases and blind spots. There are massive gaps in the skill and speed with which different people process information. Emotions can trump rationality. Simon coined the term "bounded rationality" to argue that rationality isn't boundless but *constrained*.

Error two: People don't have the resources to do a complete search. People have limited brainpower (computational constraint). People have limited time. While finding a solution, people embark on a "selective search" of the areas where they *intuit* solutions might be found.

Error three: Optimum solutions aren't realistic. Business decisions are time-sensitive; full consequences can't be known; an employee's optimum solution won't be the manager's. Therefore people don't optimize, they *satisfice*: they go for solutions that <u>satis</u>fy and suf<u>fice</u>.

Simon saw that classical economic theory missed the real-life context in which decisions are made. Limited rationality, time constraints, and misaligned "optimum solutions" are present in real-life, but absent in classical economic theory.

The Nobel Prize committee noted Simon's central insight in a special press release: "What is new in Simon's ideas is that he (replaces) the omniscient, rational, profit-maximizing entrepreneur...with decision-makers whose capacities for rational action are limited."

In his Nobel Prize acceptance lecture, Simon Herbert said humans look for solutions that are "sufficient unto the day." Humans have an "aspiration" for "how good an alternative" they should find. Once they meet an alternative that meets the initial aspiration, they terminate the search.

Herbert Simon's models on human decision-making are used by AI researchers today to code programs and develop networked computers that can learn from feedback—he continues to be the most cited researcher for AI and cognitive psychology on Google Scholar till date.

To conclude: Each human decision is haunted by limited knowledge, time-constraints, and competing interests—even among partners. Under such conditions, we look not so much for the perfect outcome, but a serviceable one. We don't *optimize*, we *satisfice*.

60

DIGGING INTO DOSTOEVSKY'S HEART

Letters of Fyodor Dostoevsky, 1914

Dostoevsky's life was a roller-coaster. He was a literary rockstar at 24 but he almost got executed by a firing squad at 28. Exiled to Siberia, he returned to write some of the greatest novels of all time, like *Crime and Punishment* and *The Brothers Karamazov*. In his lesser-known letters and essays, we get a more *intimate* look at what he loved, hated, and fiercely believed in. Dig in:

Dostoevsky believed life is only possible when you have a philosophical north star you swear by: "Neither a person nor a nation can exist without some higher idea." Dostoevsky: "In order to maintain itself and live, every society must necessarily respect someone and something." If you have scorn for everything, you have no center of gravity.

In his essay against environmental determinism, Dostoevsky wrote: "The doctrine of the environment reduces man to an absolute nonentity, exempts him totally from every personal moral duty and from all independence, reduces him to the lowest form of slavery imaginable." Is this worldview acceptable to any self-respecting man?

In a letter, Dostoevsky revealed the mystery he wanted to solve: "Man is a mystery: if you spend your entire life trying to puzzle it out, then do not say that you have wasted your time. I occupy myself with this mystery, because I want to be a man."

Dostoevsky needed only three things: "I need nothing but books, the possibility of writing, and of being daily for a few hours alone. To be alone is a natural need, like eating and drinking." Certain spiritual and intellectual problems demand solitude.

But Dostoevsky also warned against introversion: "Lacking external experiences, those of the inward life will gain the upper hand. The nerves and the fancy then take up too much room. Every external happening seems colossal, and frightens us. We begin to fear life." People today are too shy to ask the waiter for extra ketchup. Trivial tasks *feel* "colossal" because of how introverted modern lives have become.

Dostoevsky lists important questions all societies must ask: "Whom can we now consider our best people? Most importantly, where shall we find them? Who will take the responsibility for proclaiming them the best, and on what basis? Does someone need to take this responsibility?" But today, our political systems worship at the altar of equality and try to weasel their way out of these questions.

Do we possess talent or does talent possess us? Dostoevsky: "It's very rare to find a person capable of handling his gift. The talent almost always enslaves its possessor, taking him, as it were, by the scruff of the neck and carrying him off far away from his proper path."

Dostoevsky on the measure of great art: "Art is always true to reality in the highest degree...it cannot be unfaithful to contemporary reality. Otherwise it would not be art. It is the measure of true art that it is always contemporary, urgent and useful." Dostoevsky's point is that even ugly art is faithful to reality. Artists are putting urinals and rotten bananas in modern museums to mirror the disgusting modern world *outside* the museum.

Art becomes abnormal when we become abnormal: "During his life man may deviate from normality, from the laws of nature; in this case art will deviate with him. But this serves to show art's close and indissoluble link with man, its constant loyalty to man and his interests."

For Dostoevsky beauty is synonymous with health and ascending life: "Beauty is useful because man has a constant need for (his) highest ideal. If a people preserves an ideal of beauty...it means that the need for health and normality is also there." The news will lie to you, the politicians will manipulate you, but your aesthetic sense will lead you to the truth.

Dostoevsky hated the "small-souled" people who preach "contentment with one's destiny" and "modest demands from life." Dostoevsky: "Their contentment is that of cloistered self-castration." All vital souls will instinctively reject such an "insipid" existence.

61

TAKE THE SUN PILL

Letters by D.H. Lawrence, 1934

SUN by D.H. Lawrence, 1928

In D.H. Lawrence's hypnotic and powerful short story SUN (1928), Juliet, a sick woman, is prescribed sun therapy by her doctor. She starts sunbathing naked and magical changes happen in her body, psyche, and being. The "cold dark clots of her thoughts" start dissolving. Dig in:

Her sun-bathing sessions slowly turn her into an aristocrat: she develops a "contempt for human beings altogether." Why? Because they are "un-elemental" and "unsunned." When she sees people, she sees "graveyard worms" who are always "innerly cowed" and afraid of the "natural blaze of life."

Why was D.H. Lawrence obsessed with the sun? His father was a coal-miner, spending most of his time in the dark underground. Lawrence didn't want that fate. He wrote: "The sun is to us what we take from it. And if we are puny, it is because we take punily from the superb sun."

Juliet, D.H. Lawrence's character, wants other people to feel what she feels with the sun. She wants them to break out in "a gesture of recklessness and salutation." The "little civilized tension" in our brows would disappear if we let the sun in.

After her sun exposure, Juliet's feelings towards her domesticated husband change for the worse. She now feels he has a "gray city face." His "extreme moderation" annoys her. Juliet thinks of him as a zoo animal: "He had the gold-gray eyes of an animal that has been caught young, and reared completely in captivity."

For D.H. Lawrence, your conscience is your inner sun: "Conscience is sun-awareness and our deep instinct to not go against the sun." When your conscience clearly blinks red or green, you are experiencing borrowed clarity from the sun itself.

Good ideas wish to live in a well-lit, sunny mind.

DH Lawrence's problem with the middle classes? They're "sunless." Lawrence: "They have only two measures: mankind and money, they have utterly no reference to the sun." For Lawrence, life without a higher reference is "meaningless" like paper money "when the bank is broke."

An aristocrat does live by higher reference points, but there's something else to him too. He has a frenzied divine energy. D.H. Lawrence: "Being alive constitutes an aristocracy which there is no getting beyond. He who is most alive, intrinsically, is King, whether men admit it or not." All attention and loyalty go to the one who's burning with life. Increase your sun exposure. Be more alive.

Lawrence predicts a new Solar Elite: "Enough of the squalor of democratic humanity! Time to recognize the aristocracy of the sun. There will form a new aristocracy, irrespective of nationality, of men who have reached the sun. In the coming era they will rule the world."

Who's a savior? D.H. Lawrence: "Whoever can establish, or initiate a new connection between mankind and the universe, is a savior." Life tends to degenerate into "repetition, torpor, ennui, lifelessness." A savior hits refresh on "the human connection with the universe."

I love D.H. Lawrence's definition of immorality: "It is only immoral to be dead-alive, sun-extinct, and busy putting out the sun in other people."

Pro tip: Don't put out the sun in other people.

62

ON TOXIC HUMILITY

Orthodoxy, 1908

Modern streets are "noisy with taxicabs and motorcars," but that's the noise of "laziness and fatigue," not activity. If everyone walked, the streets would be quieter but more alive. Modern thought is like a modern street. A busy vibe, long words, and loud ideas are all hiding laziness underneath.

Humility can be toxic too. Chesterton contrasts old humility with new humility: "The old humility made a man doubtful about his efforts, which might make him work harder. But the new humility makes a man doubtful about his aims, which will make him stop working altogether."

"Art has no limits," screams the dullest modern artist you know. But Chesterton shows why art *requires* limitations: "The essence of every picture is the frame. If you draw a giraffe, you must draw him with a long neck. If, in your bold creative way, you hold yourself free to draw a giraffe with a short neck, you'll really find that you're not free to draw a giraffe."

Why it's anti-democratic to ignore tradition: "Tradition means giving votes to the most obscure of all classes, our ancestors. It is the democracy of the dead. Tradition refuses to submit to the small and arrogant oligarchy of those who merely happen to be walking about." But how many so-called "democrats" care about tradition at all?

Love precedes lovability: "Men did not love Rome because she was great. She was great because they had loved her." A "primary devotion" to a place, thing, or person is the source of the creative energy that transforms it. Begin with love, not scorn.

It is impossible to critique without standards. Chesterton: "When little boys in the street laugh at the fatness of some distinguished journalist, they are unconsciously assuming a standard of Greek sculpture." The modern person carries around a permanently critical mood, and yet finds standards intolerably offensive.

The paradox of fairy tales: "All the beauty of a fairy-tale lies in this: that the prince has a wonder which just stops short of being fear. If he is afraid of the giant, there is an end of him; but also if he is not astonished at the giant, there is an end of the fairytale."

How to think about the environment around us: "This is not a world, but rather the material for a world. God has given us not so much the colors of a picture as the colors of a palette. But he has also given us a subject, a model, a fixed vision."

Chesterton on the emptiness of the atheist's worldview: He has "nothing to show us except more and more infinite corridors of space lit by ghastly suns and empty of all that is divine." The assertion that the universe is ultimately meaningless is as unprovable as the assertion that it is ultimately meaningful. But while the religious assertion gives life a grand and tragic tenor, the atheist assertion makes existence a farce.

Healthy men have the bandwidth for superfluity: "It's the happy man who does the useless things; the sick man isn't strong enough to be idle." A sick man doesn't have the energy for "careless and causeless actions." But a healthy man whistles, pets the street cat, and wastes time admiring the sunset.

63

WHY YOU SHOULD DRAW
MANDALAS

Mandala Symbolism, 1972

Once upon a time, Carl Jung and Sigmund Freud were the best of friends. Jung was Freud's prodigal intellectual son and the heir to the psychoanalytic empire. But then Jung was too independent a thinker and they eventually fell out. Jung went on to invent the categories of introversion and extroversion, introduce the world to the reality of the "collective unconscious", and investigate mysterious symbols like the Indian *mandala*. Here's what Jung found about Mandalas:

In Jung's practice, his patients often produced mandalas spontaneously as "free creations of fantasy." They'd never been to India. They'd never seen a mandala in their life. Jung: "The pictures come as a rule from educated persons who were unacquainted with the ethnic parallels."

Jung wrote that in therapy, mandalas represent "a kind of new centering." The mandala expresses the client's desire for "order, balance, and wholeness." Jung: "That is why mandalas mostly appear in connection with chaotic psychic states of disorientation or panic."

Mandala, in Sanskrit, means a "circle." In religious rituals, mandalas "aid concentration by narrowing down the psychic field of vision." A mandala's role is to turn attention *inward,* hold the outside world *at bay,* and help the psyche achieve *inner coherence.*

We live a fractured existence—the mandala is a portal into becoming whole again.

Jung writes that when one engages with a mandala deeply, one experiences an "almost irresistible compulsion and urge to become what one is." The source of this feeling is the hypnotic *center* of the mandala, which points at the center of our *psyche* "to which everything is related, by which everything is arranged, and which is itself a source of energy."

Jung: "This center is not felt or thought of as the ego but as the self. Although the center is represented by an innermost point, it is surrounded by a periphery containing everything that belongs to the self—the paired opposites that make up the total personality." Life is a polar phenomenon—it requires "paired opposites" like love and hate, male and female, the conscious and the unconscious, to work. The mandala arranges such polarities around its center.

Mandalas often contain snakes. What do they stand for? Jung wrote that inside a mandala, a snake "signifies the circumambulation of, and way to, the center." To achieve psychic growth, one often has to slither through dark underground chambers and be flexible—like a snake.

Carl Jung believed that our collective human unconscious is teeming with many emotionally significant symbols. They burst to the surface in dreams. The Mandala is one such symbol—looking at it, drawing it, and studying it holds the key to many mental breakthroughs.

64

LIFE CAN'T BE PAUSED UNTIL
YOU WORK OUT ITS MEANING

Pensées , 1838

Joseph Joubert, an 18th century Frenchman, published nothing during his life. After his death, his widow released his notebooks as *Pensées* (Thoughts). The world finally recognized his aphoristic genius. Some selected insights on life, unfinished thoughts, and more:

Speed is overrated; direction underrated: "The direction of the mind is more important than its progress." It is better to go fast on the right road than to go slow, but it's the worst to go fast on the wrong road.

It is hard to judge the material world without a spiritual reference point: "We comprehend the earth only when we have known heaven. Without the spiritual world the material world is a disheartening enigma."

Abstract ideas shape history as much as concrete things like technology, weapons, and people. Joubert: "A thought is a thing as real as a cannonball."

Ideas and emotions are tied. Intellectual turmoil means emotional turmoil: "Without fixed ideas, no fixed feelings. Whoever has no constant opinions has no constant emotions." Cultivate mental clarity so you may have a pure constancy of heart.

Too much planning hurts the project: "To draw up in advance an exact and detailed plan is to deprive our minds of the pleasures of the encounter and the novelty that comes from executing the work." The execution will be more fun than the plan, so don't delay it.

Jourbert noted how different emotions manifest physically: "Pride swells the brain. Vanity carries with it smoke. Hatred tightens the heart. Love warms the lungs. Admiration stops the heart. We breathe through desire. Sadness is inaction."

Life can't be paused until you discover its true meaning: "To seek the truth...but, as you are seeking and as you are waiting, what will you *do*, what will you *think*, what will you *practice*, what rules will you *follow*?" We need to embody a philosophy, to live out a worldview, *before* we can work out all the details in theory.

Think more *finished* thoughts: "To finish one's thought! It is a long process, it is rare. It gives intense pleasure. Because every finished thought easily enters the mind. They don't have the same need to be beautiful in order to please. It is enough for them to be finished."

To master an idea, teach it: "To teach is to learn twice over."

You'll find the right words once you've worked the right ideas: "Ideas never lack for words. It is words that lack ideas. As soon as the idea has come to its last degree of perfection, the word blossoms."

65

WHY YOU NEED TO BE STUPID
SOMETIMES

Beyond Good and Evil, 1886

Nietzsche paid out of his pocket to print *Beyond Good and Evil*. It has now become one of the most popular philosophy books in history. Nietzsche asks a deep question: "What are the ideas by which one could live MORE vigorously and joyfully than by modern ideas?" He gives 9 great answers:

Too much peace can be its own form of hell. Nietzsche: "Under conditions of peace the warlike man attacks himself." War forces us to take stock of "our resources, our virtues, our shield and spear, our spirit"—and it "compels us to be strong."

The young think in absolutes—and pay a terrible price. The young "respect and despise without the art of nuance." We worship what only deserves mild affection. We reject completely what can teach us things. Nietzsche: "Introduce a little art into your feelings."

Men and women miscommunicate because they dance to DIFFERENT rhythms. Nietzsche: "The same emotions in man and woman are different in tempo: therefore man and woman never cease to misunderstand one another." Well-arranged differences in tempo, however, make a song...

Don't sacrifice your face—for your mask. "Who has not," Nietzsche asks, "for the sake of his reputation—sacrificed himself?" A uniform persona, regardless of inner change, has social benefits. But be wary. A role played long enough REPLACES the self that was playing it.

Beware of contagious shame. Nietzsche: "To be ashamed of one's immorality: that is a step on the ladder at the end of which one is also ashamed of one's morality." One starts off accepting a mistake, and soon accepts he's ALWAYS mistaken.

Make decisions, and don't waver. Nietzsche: "Close your ears to even the best counter-argument once the decision has been taken." You need this "occasional will to stupidity" if you are to ever finish the things you start.

Advice for all writers, teachers, and politicians: "The more abstract the truth you want to teach the more you must seduce the senses to it." Make your abstract ideas *characters* in a story if you can. If you can make a concept a full-body experience, people will remember it.

Find out who's the king in your inner kingdom. Among your drives, the strongest one is the monarch to whom everything else inside you will eventually bow.

Nietzsche: "To our strongest drive, the tyrant in us, not only our reason but also our conscience submits."

Act within constraints—for a long time—and you'll go far. Nietzsche: "The essential thing in heaven and upon earth seems to be a protracted *obedience* in *one* direction: from out of that there always emerges and has always emerged in the long run something for the sake of which it is worthwhile to live on earth, for example virtue, art, music, dance, reason, spirituality – something transfiguring, refined, mad and divine."

66

THE NIETZSCHE MIXTAPE

The Complete Works of Friedrich Nietzsche, 1913

This is a free-ranging curation sourced from Nietzsche's whole oeuvre. Nietzsche returned to the same themes across different books, and this curated list of 22 ideas will introduce you to them. Get ready to be struck by lightning:

Nietzsche on strength: "Only excess of strength is proof of strength." You only possess those things that you can afford to waste: Only *excessive* spending is proof of wealth. Only *needless* risk is proof of courage. Going overboard demonstrates authenticity.

Limit your information intake. Nietzsche: "Once and for all, there is a great deal I do not want to know – Wisdom sets bounds even to knowledge." We must take care that acquiring knowledge doesn't distract from acquiring power, sway, clout, and *real* domination over the *real* world.

Nietzsche on humility: "When it is trodden on a worm will curl up. That is prudent. It thereby reduces the chance of being trodden on again. In the language of morals: humility." Humility: scared animal reducing surface area. Pride: strong animal increasing surface area.

When the psyche is properly calibrated, we *instinctively* make great decisions. Nietzsche: "To have to combat one's instincts – that is the formula for décadence: as long as life is ascending, happiness and instinct are one." Reason drives a wedge between us and our gut.

Nietzsche on the complainers: "Every poor devil finds pleasure in scolding – it gives him a little of the intoxication of power. Even complaining and wailing can give life a charm for the sake of which one endures it: there is a small dose of revenge in every complaint."

Here's how not to deal with powerful desires. Nietzsche: "Castration is instinctively selected in a struggle against a desire by those who are too weak-willed, too degenerate to impose moderation." Lust, greed, wrath needn't be castrated as *sins* but rather *wielded* as weapons.

Turbulence, mental contradictions and war keep us sharp. Nietzsche: "One is fruitful only at the cost of being rich in contradictions; one remains young only on condition the soul does not relax, does not long for peace. One has renounced grand life when one renounces war."

Nietzsche saw our age coming: a time when everyone feels permanently broken. He wrote: "Here everyone helps everyone else, here everyone is to a certain degree an invalid and everyone a nurse. This is then called virtue." Stronger ages "overflowing" with life would pity such cowardice.

Nietzsche on equality: "Equality belongs essentially to decline: the chasm between man and man, class and class, the multiplicity of types, the will to be oneself, to stand out – that which I call pathos of distance – characterizes every strong age." Nobility wants to stand out.

Stop being busy. Nietzsche writes that a "raging industriousness" will give you wealth. But it will also drain you—make your senses less subtle. Work gives, but also extracts: time, energy, one's enthusiasm. Work is a trade—important to keep track of what one *gives away*.

Nietzsche predicts the internet in the 1880s? He says: In modern times, the "abundance of disparate impressions is greater than ever." But "the ability to take initiative" is lost. People are "accustomed to being overwhelmed." And all they can do is "react to external stimuli."

Nietzsche describes three modern vices.

1.   **Overwork.** To be constantly busy is self-negation. It betrays "a will to forget" oneself.
2.   **Curiosity.** Vague curiosity about everything, without deep obsessions, goes nowhere.
3.   **Sympathy.** Sympathy for all = a refusal to rank good and bad.

Nietzsche: "Whoever does not have two-thirds of his day for himself, is a slave." From the *Bronze Age Mindset (2018)*: "Leisure is the source of all great things." Bronze Age Pervert, the anonymous writer of BAM, writes one must be free from life's tedious demands for "all high science, all beautiful living, all adventures."

Religious wars as progress? Religious wars show the masses have become subtle enough "to treat concepts with respect." Religious wars are only possible when people realize that mental concepts shape physical outcomes. For Nietzsche this shows the growth of the common mind.

Male versus female genius. For Nietzsche, the female genius is *receptive*. Like an actor, female genius absorbs outside scripts *fully*. A shapeshifting talent. In contrast, the male genius is to *hold* shape. Like an architect, male genius seeks "victory over weight and gravity."

Art has become cope. Previously, all art was made to "commemorate high and happy moments." Now, Nietzsche writes, art is made to offer a "brief lustful moment" to people who are "wretched, exhausted, and sick." Art was a celebration. Now it is a fake escape.

Nietzsche on the cost of God's death: "Man has suffered an incredible loss of dignity in his own eyes." He went from playing "the central part and tragic hero in the drama of existence" to being a random mote flying through space. Without a grand story, our spirit stagnates.

Nietzsche wonders if philosophy is just "an interpretation of the body and a misunderstanding of the body." He argues that thoughts arise to justify, continue, or damage some bodily states. A pessimistic philosophy might be a tired organism's justification for its own sloth.

Nietzsche: "It requires more genius to spend than to acquire." To acquire money, you learn what's profitable and repeat it. But to spend, you must answer hard questions: *What* is worth spending on? What makes you *content*? Spending well is tougher than acquiring a lot.

Common vs Noble. Nietzsche writes that "the higher type is more unreasonable." The common people are pragmatic, and ignore their "strongest instincts"—passions are wild animals that only the noblest try to ride.

If you are internally splintered, you will grow "fainthearted and unsure." We need inner congruity—cognitive consonance, if you will— as much as we need air and food. Nietzsche writes: "If a unity of plan does not already reside in things it must be implanted into them. Thus man spins his web over the past and subdues it."

There's no such thing as art for art's sake. All art seeks to "praise," "glorify," "select," and "highlight" something. Nietzsche: "By doing all this it strengthens or weakens certain valuations." The artists making "purposeless" art? Even they are worshiping something, namely randomness and chaos.

67

IN DEFENSE OF LIMITS

The Birth Of Tragedy, 1871

Use and Abuse of History For Life, 1874

Orthodoxy, 1908

Nietzsche was the first philosopher of limits.

"The essence of every picture is the frame"—G.K. Chesterton.

Earth's gravity limits how high we can jump, but this doesn't mean the void of space provides better living conditions. The horizon limits how far the sailor can see, but no ship can sail without the horizon. Incidentally, Gravity and Horizon are also Nietzsche's metaphor for God.

When Nietzsche announced the death of God, he announced the disappearance of our moral gravity and intellectual horizon. He saw that limitless freedom would be, above all, *disorienting*. Right from his first book, he'd been writing about how limits are a friend to life...

A living body has limits, a dead body does not. Every animal strictly defends its border—its skin. Try playfully poking a tiger and see what happens. A tiger's corpse, on the other hand, allows free traffic to the elements from outside. What is dead has no limits.

<u>What limits us, empowers us.</u> Freedom can be a false God. Great achievement is often unlocked when man's consciousness is limited to a single goal. But Nietzsche wrote that it's not just individuals, but entire societies, that need limits to thrive.

In *The Birth Of Tragedy*, Nietzsche writes: "Only a horizon ringed about with myths can unify a culture." If a culture is not limited to a set of foundational myths, it has no common ground to stand on. People in a community need to share not just their language but their *stories*.

Nietzsche writes: "All living things require an atmosphere around them....a living thing can be healthy, strong and fruitful only when bounded by a horizon; if it is incapable of drawing a horizon around itself, it will pine away slowly or hasten to its timely end."

In his essay *Use and Abuse of History For Life*, Nietzsche talks about the "art and power of forgetting." Because we can forget, we can act. To do anything worthwhile requires forgetting about the past and the future—requires limiting one's awareness to the present moment.

In a lecture, Jordan Peterson noted that Batman is more interesting and (significantly more) lucrative than Superman. Why? Because Batman is human. He has limits. Superman has laser eyes, monster strength, God-like power—his limitless abilities actually make him *boring.*

An underrated aspect of success: It's a by-product of placing the right limitations on oneself. Winners are people who *restrict* themselves to a favorable mindset. They enforce a *stricter* set of values. They know distraction is freedom's dark underbelly. They befriend limits.

68

MAN'S GREAT LONELINESS

Man and Technics, 1931

Oswald Spengler voted for Hitler in 1932 but remained unimpressed with him after a personal meeting. Joseph Goebbels, the chief propagandist of the Reich, nevertheless invited Spengler to give speeches. Spengler declined. The Nazis enthusiastically cited his work—before banning it.

Spengler was invited to be the Professor of Philosophy at the University of Göttingen, but he declined this offer too. Instead he spent his time buying thousands of books, collecting ancient Turkish, Persian and Indian weapons, and writing cult bestsellers such as *Decline of the West* (1918) and *Man and Technics* (1931).

Man and Technics is shorter and denser of the two. It talks about the spiritual differences between plant life and animal life, why modern civilization is a trap, and man's great loneliness. Jump in:

Spengler explains why plants are the lower form of life: "It selects neither its position, nor its nourishment, nor the other plants with which it produces its offspring. It does not move itself, but is moved by wind and warmth and light." Plants lack agency.

Among animals, Spengler notes there are two types. There are animals who depend on the "immobile plant-world" for food, and then there are animals "whose living consists in killing." This split between herbivores and carnivores, for Spengler, has deep significance.

Carnivorous predators are the "highest form of mobile life." For them, survival is tied to "fighting and winning and destroying." To live, they must get the better of their prey, which is "itself mobile, and highly so, and moreover it is combative and well equipped with dodges."

The herbivores are innately *defensive*, the carnivores are innately *offensive*. The herbivores subsist on food that "cannot flee or defend" itself. The herbivore only has to defensively *take flight* when threatened. The carnivore, on the other hand, must strategize, attack, and destroy.

Since the two live differently, herbivores and carnivores *perceive* differently. The herbivores rely on their scent and hearing; the carnivores "rule with the eye." The nose and the ear can't give you a target—they only give you a sense of distance (between you and the predator.)

It's the eyes, chico. Herbivore eyes are "set sideways, each giving a different impression"—while carnivore eyes are set next to each other, giving the animal a *target*.

Carnivores have a "wide-angle vision" that helps them measure up the "objects and conditions" during combat.

Human eyes are clearly carnivorous. We are power-maxing apex predators.

The arrangement of the eyes we share with other carnivores. But Spengler writes we humans have something *no* other animal has. A "weapon unparalleled" in the history of life: the human hand. The human hand *creates* weapons and tools that *enhance* its power 100x—no other organic appendage can give *itself* superpowers. The hand knows hot from cold, solid from liquid—it helps us manipulate and control space.

The human eye, combined with the human hand, is the deadliest combo in the world. The eye is the observer, concerned with the *truth*. The hand is the doer, concerned with *action*. The eye "seeks out cause and effect," while the hand deals with "means and end." Humans thrive when our truth-seeking and action-seeking instincts are in a state of healthy balance.

Individuality and property are carnivorous ideas. Herbivores move in herds. Individuality is born with the carnivore, who does not tolerate "an equal in his den." Property is a "royal idea." It means the right to impose one's will on space—it belongs to the predator.

Man was born to rule, and therefore mere materialist wins never satisfy us. Some want a future without war, inequality, danger—and with endless comfort—but

Spengler writes this "Earthly paradise" won't satisfy us. "Appalling boredom" will set in, and undermine the utopia.

Spengler's complaint with modern civilization is that it is anti-freedom. As societies get more complex, everyone becomes less free. From the king to the soldier, everyone becomes a cog committed to the "enterprise, whatever it may be." You must stay "in form." You're a *prisoner* of the role, unable to take on a new *form*.

Tightly organized societies make man a caged animal. Spengler writes that the *exceptional* man rebels against the "spiritual and intellectual" shackles placed on him. He seeks an escape from civilization via different means: "lordship over it, flight from it, contempt for it." Whether a man is lording over civilization, fleeing from it, or deriding it—It's all a "reaction against" being submerged in the masses. Spengler notes that "the conqueror, the adventurer, the hermit, the criminals and the bohemian" have more in common than they think. They're all rebelling against a "safe" life from which adventure and greatness have been culled.

Sure, our species has made incredible material progress. But Spengler writes that the *why* matters more than the *what*: "What matters is not how one fashions things, but what one does with them; not the weapon, but the battle." Technological progress and material improvements are "the what." What use are all these weapons—if we don't know which battle to fight? What use are technological advancements if we are never allowed to test them beyond the social scripts we are handed out?

Spengler on the human soul: "It stands in irreconcilable opposition to the whole world, from which its own *creativeness* has sundered it. It is the soul of an *upstart*." Other animals face an immovable landscape—humans face, relatively speaking, a blank canvas. The great challenge is deciding what goes on the canvas...

Spengler writes that the best among humans never achieve "quiet, happiness, or enjoyment." They're too full of creative energies. They always get what they yearn for: new struggles against the frontier. Their creative life is a curse, but there's a "grandeur" inherent in it too.

Let's end with the Spenglerian dichotomy between aesthetes and materialists. Spengler writes that there are two broad ways of being in the world. Aesthetes value a civilization "in terms of the number of the pictures and books that it produced." They put art *above* economics, politics, and engineering. The materialists, on the other hand, place emphasis on technological advancement and prosperity. Aesthetes lack a "sense of reality," the materialists suffer from "devastating shallowness." Triangulating from this, for Spengler the ideal man is a realist poet—he has a firm grip on the world, but never so tight that all magic or nobility is squeezed out.

WORKS CITED

1. De Architectura, 30 B.C.
2. The Art of Rhetoric, 4th C B.C.
3. Poetics, 335 B.C.
4. Learning In Wartime, 1939
5. Genius: The Natural History of Creativity, 1995
6. The Architecture of Servitude and Boredom, 1981
7. The Mating Mind, 2000
8. The Problem of Evil in Fiction, 1980
9. The Maps Of Meaning, 1999
10. 12 Rules For Life, 2018
11. Sexual Personae, 1991
12. The Hedgehog and the Fox, 1953
13. The Yogi and the Commissar, 1945
14. The Elements of Style, 1918
15. Twelve Against The Gods, 1929
16. On the Use and Abuse of History for Life, 1874
17. The Futurist Manifesto, 1909
18. Moral Maxims and Reflections, 1665
19. Zen In The Art Of Writing, 1990
20. The Spirit of Romance, 1910
21. ABC of Reading, 1934
22. A Defense of Enthusiasm, 1835
23. The Aristos, 1964
24. Thoughts by Napoléon Bonaparte, 1838
25. Napoleon in his own Words, 1916
26. Mind of Napoleon, 1915

55. Recognitions: Studies on Men from the Perspective of the Right, 1974
56. Fragments, 6th century B.C.
57. The Nobel Prize in Economics, 1978 Banquet Speech
58. Letters of Fyodor Dostoevsky, 1914
59. Letters by D.H. Lawrence, 1934
60. SUN by D.H. Lawrence, 1928
61. Orthodoxy, 1908
62. Mandala Symbolism, 1972
63. Pensées , 1838
64. Beyond Good and Evil, 1886
65. The Complete Works of Friedrich Nietzsche, 1913
66. The Birth Of Tragedy, 1871
67. Man and Technics, 1931

If you enjoyed this book...

Buy a copy for a friend!

Post a review on X/Twitter (and tag me: @oldbooksguy).

Copy paste the review on Amazon.

I look forward to sharing the next book with you (It will be better.)

THE END

Made in the USA
Monee, IL
14 January 2025

76881255R00166